MY LIFE
WITH THE
GREEN & GOLD

MY LIFE
WITH THE
GREEN & GOLD

Tales from 20 Years of Sportscasting

JESSIE GARCIA

Wisconsin Historical Society Press

Published by the Wisconsin Historical Society Press
Publishers since 1855

wisconsin history.org

Photographs identified with WHi or WHS are from the Society's collections; address
requests to reproduce these photos to the Visual Materials Archivist at the Wisconsin
Historical Society, 816 State Street, Madison, WI 53706.

All photos are from the author's collection unless otherwise indicated.
Cover photo by Mark Hoffman
Page vi: Jessie changing a diaper in the Packers tunnel.
Printed in the United States of America
Designed by Brian Donahue / bedesign, inc.

17 16 15 14 13   1 2 3 4 5

Library of Congress Cataloging-in-Publication Data
Garcia, Jessie, 1970–
  My life with the green and gold : tales from 20 years of sportscasting / Jessie Garcia.
     pages cm
  Includes index.
  ISBN 978-0-87020-619-1 (pbk. : alk. paper) 1. Garcia, Jessie, 1970–2. Women sportscasters—
Wisconsin—Biography. 3. Green Bay Packers (Football team)—History. I. Title.
  GV742.42.G35A3 2013
  070.4'49796092—dc23
  [B]
                                    2013008313

♾ The paper used in this publication meets the minimum requirements of the American
National Standard for Information Sciences—Permanence of Paper for Printed Library
Materials, ANSI Z39.48-1992.

For
Paul,
Jake,
and
Charlie

CONTENTS

PROLOGUE

IT'S 5 A.M. AND I'M DRIVING through a dark Wisconsin winter morning, on my way to the airport, en route to the Super Bowl.

And I'm crying.

Why am I crying? It's Super Bowl XLV, for heaven's sake. Everybody tells me how cool that is. Cry me a river, right? An all-expenses-paid trip to Dallas for eight days. Who wouldn't love that? Some parents might clamor for a week away from their kids. Oh, I've had days like that, and I'm not downplaying the excitement of the assignment—the pinnacle for sportscasters. But I am more than a sportscaster: I'm a mom, and right now all I can think about is how I peeked into my seven-year-old son's bedroom before I snuck out the door, his body flailed to the side, taking up an entire double bed, wavy hair on a Spiderman pillow. My eleven-year-old was tucked into the top bunk in his room, sports pennants taped and tacked to his walls as his straighter hair rested on a plain blue, more adult, pillowcase. I had slept on the living room couch so as not to disturb anyone. At 4:30 a.m. I was tiptoeing around the house, leaving a note on the kitchen table that said "I LOVE YOU!" and easing my way out the back door and into an arctic blast of air, a bagel

1

in my hand, a week's worth of clothes dragging behind me.

This is the yin and yang of motherhood, the balance I'm constantly trying, and usually failing, to achieve. Maybe I'm just emotional because I only slept two hours (fitfully, eye on the clock), knowing I had to catch a plane to Denver to catch a plane to Dallas and be ready to "hit the ground running," as people in the news business like to say. But I know it's more because I have already been gone from the house way too much in recent weeks during the frantic buildup to the Super Bowl. In fact, I've hardly been home.

"You're not leaving *again*?" my seven-year-old wails, hanging onto my leg with all of his first-grade strength.

"We need you in Green Bay" is the constant refrain from my bosses.

I live in Milwaukee. One hour and forty-five minutes door-to-door to Lambeau Field. Two hours if you stop at the Hardee's in Sheboygan. I'm the host of *The Mike McCarthy Show*. I need to interview the coach every week. Not to mention the constant coverage the station thinks we need to provide.

"Feed the beast," the reporters joke with each other.

But no one expected *this* team to get to the big game. Just a few weeks ago I was still telling my mom, "Don't worry, there's no way they're going to the Super Bowl." She's concerned because she won't be in the state to babysit. She has to travel to the East Coast to help my aunt who's going through chemotherapy.

My reasoning was based on some facts. The team was young, with hardly anyone on board with Super Bowl experience. They were injured, starter after starter going down. But as I watched from across the room as Aaron Rodgers, in his gray suit, straightened his tie in the locker room to take the captain's picture, I started to have a premonition. There was a bounce in their step, something special about this group. Don't they always say the team that's most on a roll will win the Super Bowl? Defying all logic they marched magically through elimination game after elimination game. They were on course to be in the NFC championship. I had been sent to the Bears-Seahawks tilt at Soldier Field the week before. Winner would take on Green Bay. Chicago prevailed, but the players were so flat in the locker room. I walked out and said to my photographer, "Man, if McCarthy can motivate the troops one ounce, they've got this one." The Bears did nothing to convince me they wanted anything less than to go home, giving us quotes about being tired and looking forward to a few days off before their next contest. When I asked about playing their archrival the Packers in the NFC title game for the first time, most didn't seem to realize that was the case, or appeared not to care.

We did a funny piece in the parking lot, asking fans who they would rather have as their quarterback, Rodgers or Jay Cutler.

"Cutler!" screamed a burly guy in a Bears sweatshirt so his friends could hear. Then he leaned in closer to the camera. "Is anyone listening?" He whispered, "Rodgers."

"You can't ask us that question. It's not fair!" said a female fan holding a beer, blond pigtails peeking out of a Bears hat.

They knew who the better quarterback was.

And so it goes. The Packers beat the Bears and we're suddenly on a Super Bowl whirlwind. They are captivating the country, the newest "America's team." It is much like the mid-'90s, when I covered two Super Bowls. But now I have two kids. Back then I could find someone to feed the cat and be off. Now here I am wiping tears from my eyes. My stomach has a pit in it. It's only eight days, I tell myself. Eight days. Yet my younger child had clung to me so tightly when I tucked him in the night before. My older son claims to be so excited about the Packers he doesn't care if he sees me or not, but I know somewhere in that jaded sixth-grade heart he will miss me. I figured out Skype and bought my first 3G card, now tucked into my briefcase. Both will help. Eight days. You can do this.

I drive to the airport, frost on the windows, and park our Honda CR-V, wondering if I will see my car, my house, my kids again. Whenever I fly fear grips me, a condition that has gotten monumentally worse since becoming a mother. My palms are always damp as I walk down any airport ramp. I see the headline: "Flight (whatever I'm on) to (wherever I'm going) Crashes." Not to mention there is a ripple of real worry about terrorism. I mean, what better place to attack America than its iconic sporting event? I will spend the week on edge, eyeing people suspiciously, while simultaneously chastising myself for profiling. Maybe the most American-looking guy in the coat and tie is the true madman.

How can one tell?

When I'm not suspecting people of misdoings, I'm thinking about the amount of work I know is ahead. What the other moms (and especially dads) don't realize when they tell me how jealous they are, is that it's actually sixteen-hour days with dinner being a granola bar from the PDQ. Our station is going all out despite the fact that we're not the network carrying the game, sending every one of the on-air sports reporters, myself included, as well as news anchors, photographers, a producer, and engineers. We are expected to turn out fresh material for three newscasts and two special segments each day. They want us live from different locations. Everything in Dallas is so spread out, we will spend hours in the car just trying to get to these different locations— and often getting lost. The weather is supposed to be bad.

My husband, Paul, will be home with our boys, Jake and Charlie. Yet he has to work, too, so we need to find a sitter to pick them up from school every day. Our college sitter can only do it for two days. I need to lean on friends. I call on my best buddies. Could they each take one day? I exhale when they say yes. Keys are passed around, arrangements made. Of course we don't count on a monster midwestern snowstorm that traps the kids at my friend Julianne's house overnight. My husband is a photographer at our TV station, WTMJ. When bad weather hits, he's expected to spring into action and stand in the snow for hours upon hours, shooting video and live shots and telling people to stay inside and be warm. Yes, it's dripping with irony. He gets nailed with work and has to snowblow two feet of white powder as a bonus when he gets home. The kids stay the night with Julianne and two of her sons.

The next day, lo and behold, is a snow day. Perfect, just perfect. No school. What now? Another friend, Kathy, was going to watch them *after* school. How would she feel about essentially having them *all day*? Paul gets the kids from Julianne's, takes them to Kathy's, and goes back to work to do more snow stories. Kathy and her husband spend the day sledding and supervising snowball fights with a gaggle of boys. I call them to apologize for invading their day and their refrigerator with two extra kids.

"It's really no problem," she tries to reassure me. I'm sure she can hear the angst in my voice. "Do you want to talk to Charlie?"

"Yes!"

He runs to the phone and I can imagine him ripping his boots off at the door, his cheeks flushed with cold and excitement.

"Hi, Mommy, we're having fun. Are you?"

I put on a brave voice and say, "Yes, but I miss you."

"When are you coming home?"

"The day after the game, honey. The day after the game."

Then he is scrambling a hasty good-bye and yelling to the other kids, "Coming..."

The kids are OK, I breathe. The kids are OK.

My other friend, Sarah, is a taskmaster. She picks up her kids, picks up mine, probably runs eight errands, teaches two Spanish classes, and has burgers going on our stove when Paul gets home another night.

"Hi, honey," she yells jokingly when he opens the door.

It all works, but I feel guilty. In fact, I feel guilty the entire week. The entire month, let's make it. I'm supposed to be part-time, but I get pulled into a more-than-full-time mix whenever something big is happening. And this is as big as it gets.

I know I owe my friends. I have great girlfriends, but it should be me making the burgers. Well, maybe not burgers. I'm a vegetarian and have never once actually cooked an edible meat dish other than hot dogs. But I could be making *something*.

Instead, I am starving in Dallas. We don't get back to the hotel until after midnight every night. This hotel seems to be located in the middle of absolutely nothing, although it sits in downtown Dallas. There is not an open restaurant or bar within a ten-mile radius except for the lobby bar, a typical sports-themed burger joint. It's as loud as can be and packed with hungry journalists.

"Don't go in there," a colleague warns me. "You'll never get your food."

I find myself in the larger-than-my-house-but-isn't-everything-bigger-in-Texas, all-night gift shop more often than I care to remember.

Hmm . . . Twinkies? No way. Those sugar-laden blueberry muffins wrapped in plastic? Ugh . . . not much better . . . empty calories, and they look like they've been on three semis on their way to the gift shop. I settle on a bag of peanuts and a V8 nearly every night. The one time I try room service, I have to call three times and wait nearly two hours for the knock on the door. I'm eating my fingernails off by the time my cheese and mushroom pizza arrives.

"Sorry, we're a little busy with this being the media hotel and all," the waiter explains.

Great.

I devour the pizza, take an Ambien, and try to enjoy the experience, while at the same time counting down the days until I can be home, eating my own food and hugging my kids.

GIRL REPORTER

I THINK BACK ON MY LIFE and wonder how I got here. How did I, with two parents with not a shred of appreciation for sports in their genes, come to be a Super Bowl reporter? Did I have a lot of brothers? Nope, only child. Did my dad at least try to throw a football with his daughter in the backyard? Never. He could not have cared less about sports; he also became an absentee father when I was still in preschool. I grew up playing with Barbies and miniature glass animals and wanting to be an actress or a veterinarian, with only my mom as support. Sports had zero place in our lives.

I'm a true American mutt. My mother, Judith Marilyn Savit, is Jewish American, born and raised in a middle-class family on Long Island. My maternal grandmother was a schoolteacher and my grandfather a daily commuter to Manhattan to work in the thread business. They expected my mother to marry a Jewish man, and I'm sure they firmly believed she would also stay right there on Long Island. What they never foresaw was her meeting David Jesus Garcia, a Mexican Catholic from the poor north side of Chicago with a mother who was a part-time nurse and a father who worked at a Chevy parts store and went scrapping in his spare time.

My father was only twenty-one and my mother twenty-five when I came along. They got married when she was pregnant. My New York, Jewish grandparents were horrified and actually disowned my mother. Wrote her right out of the will, pretended she didn't exist. It was a terrible time for my mom. It was only after I was born that her parents started to warm up. They wanted to meet their granddaughter. My mom flew with me to New York. Things got civil but hurt feelings were never repaired.

My mother jokes that she still can't believe I'm a sportscaster, but I think it fits all of my interests (OK, minus the veterinarian). There is some acting and performance involved; I always loved writing and interviewing; and it's an unusual job for women—something my mother taught me about by being a carpenter and architectural designer in the 1970s. My dad is an ex-hippie who boasts about having tear gas thrown on him. My parents settled in Madison when my mom chose to go to grad school there. I was born five days after Sterling Hall was bombed on the University of Wisconsin–Madison campus as part of an antiwar protest. My mother could see the shell of the building from her hospital bed. Then my father cheated and the divorce followed shortly. My dad drifted away from us, eventually settling in Arkansas. Luckily my mom would meet a kind man when I was ten. It was Howard who started to show me how much fun sports could be.

I was a terrible athlete. People think I must have been a star player to have become a sports reporter, but the truth is, I stood in right field in softball praying with every pitch that the ball wouldn't come my way. I joined my high school track team and for some unknown reason the coach decided I should try hurdles.

"Just run and leap over it," he tells me. I build up my courage as he sets a hurdle to the lowest point. But when I get to it, I panic and can't leap. Instead, I run right through the hurdle, knocking it and myself over. My coach tells this story at the track banquet later that year.

I never fully master hurdles, but I enjoy solitary sports and always have known I was a writer. I make stories up in my head while walking home from school; for example, "The Adventures of Q" was my first mystery story. That summer after third grade I sit on a towel at B.B. Clarke Beach with my friend Joanna, and she asks me to tell her tales.

Or sometimes we decorate a make-believe mansion in our heads. She would lie there with her eyes closed while I created each room with words. I start carrying a tape recorder around with me—the big, bulky, 1980s version—taking it to the grocery store and describing everything: the plums, the milk, what the checker looks like. I interview my mom, her friends, the cat.

Journalism seemed to be in my blood but sports certainly weren't. In 1982 the Brewers go to the World Series, but I am still an oblivious twelve-year-old. We've gone camping near Milwaukee and we're driving home through the heart of down-town, right by Marquette University, the night fans are in the streets scream-ing and waving towels around in celebration, but I still don't get it.

"What's going on?" I ask Howard.

"The Brewers are going to the World Series!"

"Oh." I had no idea.

The reason I finally get into sports is that the crowd I hang around with in high school likes them. We watch Brewers games and Badgers basketball

A true 1970s Madison kid: at the Mifflin Street block party with my mom

games, and I date a couple of golfers, one of them the future brother-in-law of professional golfer Steve Stricker. But football is still not on my radar. I join the cheerleading squad and, yes, I'm at plenty of football games, but I'm not paying much attention. We're more interested in wearing the cute purple and gold skirts and coming up with creative cheerleading mounts. One of our cheerleaders, Meghan Reek, is funky and different. She wants us to create asymmetrical mounts, not all perfectly formed like the suburban girls would do. We're the low-rent east-siders. She goes on to work in fashion in San Francisco, but for now we're so busy bending, twisting, and standing on each other's backs per her orders, we forget to watch the action.

"Are we on offense or defense right now?" is heard more often from the cheerleaders than it should be.

East High School has powder-puff football at homecoming. The girls get to play and are coached by the guys. At halftime we line up and listen to the team's running back as he instructs us and draws plays with one of his right fingers on the palm of his left hand.

"Each player has a number and each hole in the offensive line has a number. So if I call out 31 that means the number 3—the running back—goes through the 1 hole."

Who would have thought this inattentive cheerleader (with friend Meghan Reek) would one day host NFL coaches' shows?

That doesn't sound too hard. My friend Mirah is a great athlete and immediately volunteers to be the running back. But I'm not a fan of contact, even in powder-puff football. I prefer to be a free safety, roaming the field and only going to the action when warranted. My days of actually playing football are limited to that one exhibition at halftime.

In AP English we're assigned to find a career we're interested in and spend the day job shadowing. My friend Gavin and I both choose TV. My uncle, one of my dad's brothers, is a producer-director at a station in Madison. He helps us follow the *Live at 5* anchors for a few hours and watch the show off to the side while it airs.

The last segment is supposed to feature a guest who has not shown up and they have time to fill.

"Let's ask these nice high school kids to come and sit in the chairs with us and talk for a few minutes," says Beth Zurbuchen, the very pleasant female anchor. Gavin and I look at each other. We're going to be on *now*?

"Come on," urges Beth. "We don't bite."

So when the last segment comes back from commercial there are two very nervous-looking high schoolers sitting in the chairs. Beth introduces us and tells the audience we are there to job shadow.

"I guess we can tell everyone that your uncle Andy Garcia is our director today," says Beth. "Having him in the business and following us—does it make you want to run away to another career?"

"No, it makes me want to do it even more," I say. My heart is pounding being on the show and I'm amazed I can form words at all. Beth asks Gavin a question about AP English, and then it's time to say good-bye. She and her coanchor, Mark Koehn, are so smooth. I'm thinking: could I ever be that comfortable?

When we leave the station and drive the twenty minutes back to our part of town, Gavin opens the window and yells, "We were just on *Live at 5*! We were just on *Live at 5*!" at the top of his lungs to every passerby.

My uncle later asks me to shoot a few lines for a series of public service announcements they are doing. I still remember my part: "Did you know that Langdon Street was named after one of the signers of our Constitution? John Langdon was a merchant from New Hampshire. His ships were used to fight British vessels in the Revolution." I deliver this in my singsongy high school voice, standing on the UW–Madison campus right in front of the Memorial Union. It's exciting, and I'm feeling that a career path is revealing itself.

My mother marries Howard and he has more of a passion for sports than any adult who's been in my life so far. We go bowling and knock a tennis ball around. He takes me to a Brewers game and explains how the outfielders are shading left and right according to the scouting report.

I turn my attention to the Madison East High School newspaper, writing all kinds of articles, with topics ranging from "What's a Purgolder?" (the school mascot that is sort of half-dog, half-bear), to a UW campus racism protest, to a political debate where we got in to see presidential candidate George H. W. Bush. But I find politics and protests not my style. The few sports stories I write are much more fun. I start to experiment with adjectives and punchy words. I know my path will be journalism and I'm sure it will be at Northwestern University in Evanston, Illinois.

Except it's not.

Despite impassioned pleas from them in search of "highly qualified Hispanic students," I am ultimately rejected, my SAT scores not good enough or my extracurriculars not impressive enough. I'm heartbroken and thinking, now what? UW–Madison is too close to home. I had applied at Boston University, a school we stumbled upon while taking a tour of East Coast cities my junior year. I was not even aware they had a good journalism school until we jumped on the last tour of the day. Suddenly BU seems like it might be the best fit. When the acceptance letter arrives, I whoop with joy.

I pack my bags and head to Boston, a slightly overwhelmed eighteen-year-old in a big city. My mom will tell me later she cried all the way to Cleveland on the drive home. I cry the first night, too, sitting on my bunk bed in a brownstone-turned-dorm next to the Charles River thinking, "Why did I leave my comfort zone?" But it turns out to be a great decision. I join *The Daily Free Press*—the school's newspaper—and request to be assigned to sports. There is one other woman, a tough cookie who will eventually run the department. I'm sent to cover the women's swimming team. Thinking I'm clever, I start to write, using all kinds of water word play ("They really dunked them today, they dove right in, they splashed to the surface"). The coach's name, no joke, is Ray Whetmore. It helps my puns. I look back now and wince, but I was trying to find my voice. In one piece I write "They did it with more style than this month's *Vogue*" and Coach Whetmore compliments me.

"The girls all loved your *Vogue* comment."

I walk around on air all day—the girls! They loved my *Vogue* comment! I try to forget the fact that he said nothing of all of my water metaphors.

I move on to rugby (I know nothing about it and have to ask what a scrum is), to lacrosse (another thing we don't have much of in Wisconsin), to basketball, and eventually find my calling in hockey. Here's a midwestern sport I enjoy. I cover the BU Terriers as they travel to places like Rensselaer Polytechnic Institute and UMass–Lowell. The coach, the legendary Jack Parker, is great and puts up with a cub reporter who probably asks a lot of dumb questions. I love the sound of the hockey arena, the puck hitting the boards and the crowd ringing cowbells. I love carrying a reporter's notebook and having a deadline to meet. I love staying up late putting the sports section together, typing madly and laying out the copy. The highlight of the experience is covering the Beanpot hockey tournament at the Boston Garden and sitting in the decrepit old press box where you have to duck your head to get in. The Garden smells like beer and peanuts. I feel like a real, actual, legitimate professional.

One semester, I jump at the chance to try an internship at a Boston TV station. It's a huge operation, the ABC affiliate, and I have my ups and downs. It is, literally, one of those stations where someone might say, "Hey, intern, can you grab those scripts for me?" It's not a very personal or warm environment.

I get yelled at for putting the list of CGs (names that appear on the screen over an interview) in the wrong place. This brings tears to my eyes until a producer talks me off the ledge, saying that everyone makes mistakes and adding that they really should have a better system in place anyway.

I ask for and am allowed a chance to follow a sports reporter to a basketball practice at Northeastern University, but he ignores me the whole time and is icy cold back at the station. I can tell he's not high on women doing sports.

I ask the 6:00 p.m. producer if I can write a "bump," which is the tease leading to the next segment. The story is about a football team from Cape Cod that has to take a ferry to the mainland for every game. I labor over this bump for an hour, finally writing something bulky like, "They are the kings of the land and the sea. They are the mighty Knights, but they have to travel far and wide." The producer takes one look and changes it to "The Cape Cod Knights . . . where getting there is half the battle." Sometimes less is more, I'm learning.

A friend of mine is a budding political campaign manager. He organizes a series of interviews with local congressional candidates and asks me to moderate. It's going to be held at Cape Cod Cable, or C3TV, as it's called. I use my waitressing money to comb the racks at Goodwill and buy something that looks TV-anchorish. I study my notes. I have to ask the candidates questions about a new sewer system and school district rezoning. This turns out to be another reminder that hard news does not hold much interest for me.

Later, a classmate asks me to do voice-over work (which she calls "easy money"). I go to a suburban Boston studio and wait to deliver my one line: "The New England Home for Little Wanderers." It's a public service announcement about a safe house for kids. They're using a young actress to play the little wanderer. She looks like a rich kid with a stage mom until they put her in a torn shirt, have her hold a scruffy teddy bear, and ask her to begin with her head down and then slowly and forlornly to look up at the camera. They even mess her hair and rub a little soot around for emphasis. *Now* she's a wanderer. I'm a little disturbed by this process, by watching her do this over and over again and then quickly remove her ripped shirt to put on a bejeweled T-shirt and brush her hair right back into place. And she's whining to her mother about how many takes she has to do.

I have to wait hours for my part. Finally, I deliver it in what I think is my most heartfelt voice. Not good enough. They not only don't think I sound sad enough, they don't like the way I say *wanderers* either. They think I have too much of a midwestern accent. I rehearse and rehearse how to say *wanderers* in a more New England manner. Their way is like *wunderers*. Mine sounds like *wonderers*. I know they're not happy. They're probably "wondering" why I was picked for this job in the first place. I leave after about fifty takes and think that voice-over work is tedious and frustrating.

We all need to interview a professional in our field for one of my communications classes. The person I admire most is a female *Boston Globe* reporter. I'm ecstatic when she agrees to meet me at Dunkin' Donuts on her way to Celtics practice. We sit, on a rainy morning, at a corner table and I interview her over coffee in Styrofoam cups. She is very easygoing and tells me about her upbringing and how she came to love sports. She asks me to send her a copy of the finished product after I write it. I do and I'm anxious to get her feedback, but I never hear a word. Meeting her taught me two valuable lessons: never be too busy to talk with a student and always respond when someone asks you to critique his or her work. It smarted that I got no reaction from her, but I was too intimidated to call and press her.

In the meantime, I take news reporting and carry the bulky VHS camera out to Fenway Park to do a story. The Red Sox are out for the season and I call the PR department to see if we can shoot a standup in the empty stadium. To my amazement they say yes and my friend and I take turns aiming the camera at each other in the stands and saying lines for our stories, in awe of the place we are occupying. Another year, one of my college roommates is working in the Red Sox ticket office and scores us seats to a postseason game against the A's. The Sox lose, but the atmosphere is so electric I know I'm hooked. Who would want to cover boring school board meetings when you could do this? My dorm room is about a five-minute walk from Fenway, and we wind up there more than we should (Studying? What's that?), thinking we're cool by buying cheap cigars at CVS and puffing on them in the bleachers.

I know I've found my career. I never waver from my major or my determination. I think back to the moment I discovered I was hooked on news. I was sixteen years old when the space shuttle *Challenger* blew up. I was home sick and in the shower with the radio on. When the announcer broke in with the news I froze, the soap in my hands. I scrambled out of the water, grabbed a towel, and ran to the living room TV. I didn't turn it off for the next ten hours. I was suddenly a news junkie. There is a feeling many news people will describe as a sense that you need to be there, need to be in the know and telling the world the details. It's an adrenaline rush. That day was my first time experiencing this.

The summer before my senior year I take another internship, this time back home in Madison at the WISC television station. My sports director is Van Stoutt, a local legend. He reads oodles of high school scores every Friday night during football and basketball seasons. There is a high school named Argyle, and Van has a running joke of using the word *sock* anytime he talks about them: "Argyle *socks* Pecatonica (or whoever they play)." He is old school.

"Who's the Paul Newman on prompter?" he yells, gesturing to the just-graduated kid running the teleprompter. We all look at each other, confused. Van explains in an exasperated tone.

"Paul New-man, the NEW man?" That's just Van. Ironically, the new man *is* named Paul and he will eventually be my husband.

I'm sent on my first solo assignment. I have to go to Wausau, in the middle of the state, for the high school baseball tournament. I'm meeting a photographer there.

At the baseball diamond the reporters sit in a dusty, field-level press area watching the contest. There is a male reporter from a competing station next to me. Just to refresh my memory on keeping score I draw a picture of a baseball diamond and label each position in the margins of my program: 1 is pitcher, 2 catcher, and so on. He must see me doing this because he tries to act casual when he asks later if he can glance at my program. He conveniently seems to have misplaced his. I see him flip through the pages until he finds my crib notes. He smirks.

"There's an idiot girl for you. She doesn't even know the numbers by heart," I'm sure he's thinking.

"Jerk" is what I think. (Actually, I was thinking something stronger, but we want to keep this clean.)

The game goes into extra innings and it's getting late. We shoot interviews and my heart is racing as I push the limits of the speedometer all the way back to the station. It's 10:10 when I come bursting through the door. I have less than ten minutes to write and edit this piece for Van's sportscast.

"You can do it," he says. I do. It airs. Maybe not a beautiful piece, but a piece nonetheless—with video and audio and a score and interviews.

Van and the other sports anchor, Jeff Lenzen, give me freedom to write all sorts of copy for them. They give me wings. It's the opposite of the Boston station, where union rules would have prohibited me from even touching the eject button on a tape machine. Here, I can edit, shoot, and practically go on the air as an intern.

We all adopt Van's favorite saying—"Good enough for sports"—every time we finish putting a story together. Despite his seemingly old-style ways he appears to have no problem with my being a woman. There are no female sports anchors in the entire state but I beg and plead for a job after college, bombarding the news director with postcards when I get back to Boston for my final year of school ("I'm cheap!" "I'll work crazy hours!"). I help them out when the Badgers hockey team plays in Providence, Rhode Island. Lying, I tell them that, sure, I have a car I can use. In reality, I use all of my money to ride the T to the airport to rent one. I drive to Providence alone and meet a nice husband-and-wife photographer team who shoot the game from the stands, then let me take over doing interviews in the locker room. This feels very important. I ask every player about ten too many questions just to be sure I'm not forgetting anything. I grab the tape and race back to Boston to WBZ-TV, a place I'm not familiar with downtown. They bring me to the feed room, a windowless space filled with television monitors; red blinking lights; and humming, buzzing tape machines. My work is being beamed back to Madison. Interviews I did are going to be on the news in my hometown that night! I'm over the moon but now also broke. I'm hoping my eagerness will pay off in the end.

Senior year I take a class on sports management. My professor is a sports agent who does a fine job teaching the class but starts to get on my nerves when he finds out I have a small connection to the Badgers hockey team. There is a player on the team he's hoping to sign, so he asks me to ask the player if he'll call him so they can talk. I barely know the Badgers and I'm pretty swamped trying to figure out my own life. The agent calls me several times to see if I've had a chance to connect with Badger X yet. He seems mildly annoyed when I say I haven't. Finally, I stop taking his calls and he leaves me alone. I don't know if he ever signed the guy he wanted, but the whole experience turned me off to ever becoming a sports agent. Working for commission is not what I want to do.

As graduation draws near, I'm still trying to land my first job—ideally back in my hometown. Was Madison, Wisconsin, ready for a non-male person reading sports to them? I'm not sure of the consensus, but WISC general manager David Sanks and news director Tom Bier think so and take a chance, hiring me to work part time. I will always be grateful to them. There could not have been a better place to start a career.

In that first year, I'm still trying to find my writing style. I'm sent to do a story on an old couple who love to bowl—this is Madison, Wisconsin, after all. We also have the hole-in-one club and the 300 club.

"Mary loves to knit in her spare time, but that doesn't mean she doesn't have *time* for a *spare*," I write. I'm still a little cheesy, but I'm getting there . . . slowly.

At first I am told I will be reporting only, but that lasts less than a month. Van is sick and they call me at home. How would I like to anchor tomorrow? I'm so nervous. I still have no money for real TV clothes. As a part-timer I have to buy my own clothes and makeup. Eventually, I would get a clothing allowance and turn in receipts for hair and makeup; as a trade-off, anchors had to receive approval for any style change and were highly encouraged to follow the advice of image consultants and makeup experts brought in by the station. I borrow an outfit from a friend and sweat through a heart-pounding first show.

I'm never truly comfortable on TV during those early years. Someone tells me just to smile a lot and no one will notice, so I do—probably way too much. One of the news anchors advises me to take scripts home and practice reading them again and again. I repeat the same sentences over and over with different inflections, trying to find a zone that feels right to me.

A few months into my career I take a phone call after the 6:00 p.m. show. A man says, "I will never watch Channel 3 again."

"Why?" I ask, genuinely baffled.

"Because you're a *chick* and chicks don't know anything about sports." I'm so stunned I stammer, "I hope you change your mind one day," and hang up. It's my first taste of real criticism for my gender. Family and friends tell me to ignore it, but I feel affronted.

This is 1992 and there aren't very many role models at this time, although I do look up to Robin Roberts at ESPN and Lesley Visser at CBS Sports. Both know their stuff and always look polished on the air, but female sportscasters are few and far between. Later in my career I will have a chance to meet both of them in person. Roberts spoke at a banquet I attended celebrating women in sports. She was funny and warm, and I liked her immediately. She was already a *Good Morning America* anchor by this time but had no airs about her as she told the audience great stories about her childhood and her days playing basketball. She remains a role model, as does Visser, who always gave me a warm smile and a big hello.

I experience my first brush with athlete-flirting while at WISC. The Packers are in town to play at UW–Madison's stadium, Camp Randall. After the game, as we head into the locker room to gather footage, one of the players says to me, "Hey, babe. Interview for a phone number," while pulling a sweatshirt over his head.

"Come on," I retort.

"I'm kidding. But you could give it to me if you want," he says with a sly smile. I shake my head and start the interview. He checks back into cool player mode and starts answering the questions. Years later I will see him at many Packers events. Clearly our little conversation was a blip in his life, yet signified so much in mine. Male athletes can and do flirt with female reporters and, yes, probably vice versa. It's a fine line I'm going to have to be careful of throughout my career.

A hard reality in fact checking comes when I accidentally say the wrong person had the longest hitting streak in the majors. No one calls to complain, but a pushy print reporter from the local paper is all over it. "Where Have You Gone, Joe DiMaggio?" is the headline to the story he writes, and he calls demanding an explanation. All I can tell him is I was looking at the wrong chart and I made a mistake, but the tone of his voice and the article is clear. A *real* sports reporter would know that in a heartbeat.

I'm still enjoying the job and observing some top-notch writing. Joel DeSpain, the crime beat reporter, does a story on a fire. The opening was, "One red shoe. That's all that was left in this devastating house fire." The video, of course, showed one red shoe in a pile of ashes. Back in college, my News Writing and Reporting professor, a crusty old *Boston Globe* reporter with a bulbous nose, had taught us a whole different way. He insisted that the only correct path to writing a story about a fire is to write the first paragraph about the dead, the second about the injured, and the third about the driven out. There would be no fancy words, no attempting to be cute or clever in his world.

"The chowda head on the Green Line [subway] doesn't want your fancy words," he would say in his thick Boston accent. "The chowda head just wants to know how many are dead, how many are injured, and how many are driven out."

But my mind is expanding. I'm seeing that there are ways to write scripts and stories that do not involve just the facts, ma'am, laid out in such a simplistic way. Joel's red shoe has influenced my work to this day.

I'm handed a camera and sent out to shoot high school football every Friday. The batteries keep dying, so we need to travel with a huge bag of extras, the bulky bag and heavy camera weighing on each shoulder as I learn how to follow the action through the lens. When I get back to the station I'm expected to edit my own pieces.

Reggie Jackson is in town and I get to do a one-on-one interview with him. Remember—I'm just ten years removed from not even knowing that the Brewers were in the World Series. I'm aware that Jackson is "Mr. October" but I'm unsure of what to ask him, so I consult with my stepdad.

"I would ask him how he wants to be remembered by his grandchildren," Howard tells me. It turns into a nice interview, but I'm also seeing that I need to be able to do this on my own. My not having a sports upbringing means it's going to take some time to get up to speed, but I'm in a career now. I can't fake it and I don't have a lot of time. So I start cramming on sports. I ask Paul all sorts of questions about things I don't understand. I look up rules in *The New York Times Guide to Spectator Sports*. I watch every game I can find and slowly I feel the knowledge coming. It's like learning a foreign language, and I get more and more comfortable with each passing home run or touchdown.

We do tons of stories on bowlers and golfers. To make it look like a bowling ball is rolling down the lane we "flip" the camera over again and again all the way from the beginning of the lane down to the bowling pins, then take the video and speed it up, over and over, until it looks like you're seeing things from the bowling ball's perspective. To reenact someone's hole in one, we have them tee off, then we roll the ball into the cup from just outside of the camera shot, only to cut back to a shot of them jumping around and celebrating.

I'm working the night shift and weekends and making $20,000 a year, but I'm having a blast.

Van is the host of *The Barry Alvarez Show* and lets me do feature stories on the UW Badgers players. For one story we interview the trainer about how the team works out and for another we get to see the huge amounts of food provided for them. Coach Alvarez drives to the station every week in his Cadillac.

"Here comes Uncle Barry," Van will say as we watch Alvarez steer the giant car slowly and carefully to its parking place.

WISC is not a tiny operation, but one night no one is there to run the audio board when a tornado warning is happening. They are going to do a cut-in. The director gives me about the fastest crash course in an audio board there is, and I nervously hover my finger over the button, probably pushing too hard when she gives me the cue. But it works! Katy Sai's audio is being broadcast over the airwaves and I'm partially responsible. Once again I feel the magic of TV.

"Jessie, meet Paul. Paul, Jessie. You're going to the state soccer tournament together," says the assignment editor, Neil Heinen. My first thought upon meeting my future husband is, "Paul. Remember the name. Paul." I'm horrible with names and don't want to look foolish with this new photographer.

As we drive to and from the soccer tourney we chat and I think to myself, "This guy is cute. And funny." We seem to have the same taste in music and movies and he's easy to hang out with. He's got brownish hair and green eyes and is from Minnesota. He likes hockey, so we talk a lot about BU hockey. I feel comfortable with him. That night while he's on the floor crew running studio camera, I'm sitting off to the side watching the show. During the commercial break he looks at me and pantomimes you-me-drink. I smile. He's asking me on a date! I nod yes as the commercial ends and he's back to running the camera. But then a sudden cold thought runs through me. I forgot I had agreed to meet another guy that night—someone I don't know well, whom I met on a train in France when I was studying abroad the previous semester. We found out we were both from Madison and agreed to try to connect again. What do I do? I want to go out with Paul but my twenty-one-year-old self can't figure out how to make this work. Years later we will laugh about how I bounced from one bar to the other, across the street from each other, telling each guy that I was out with coworkers and "people you don't know . . . I'll be *right* back," before heading to the other bar. Eventually I shake the train guy and focus on Paul. We drink at an

Irish pub on State Street and he asks me what happened to my knee. I have a big Band-Aid on.

"Oh, I was playing tennis and I tripped over a loose ball," I say. This is a fabrication. I actually was jogging in the neighborhood and fell over my own two feet, but I feel dumb. Maybe a tennis ball sounds slightly less clumsy? He nods. After we're comfortably married I will tell him this story and we can chuckle that I lied to him twice on our first date.

He walks me to my car and we kiss in the parking lot. I now have a workplace romance on my hands. We're soon engaged, much to the shock of my parents ("You're only twenty-one. Are you crazy?"). But Paul comes from solid stock, I can tell. He calls me Root Beer (brown eyes), I call him 7UP (green eyes). We're going to get hitched, but we promise our parents we'll have a long engagement and get to know each other better. His parents are a little taken aback that we actually move in together before getting married. Plus, they're Catholic. I'm not. Another mixed marriage in the family. At least no one disowns anyone. My Jewish grandfather considers boycotting the wedding (this is the man who offered me a new car in college if I married a Jew). In the end he's there. We use a judge to officiate a ceremony in an old converted barn-turned-restaurant in Verona and we're married.

After two years in Madison, Paul New-man and I start to branch out. We look at Chicago, Minneapolis, and eventually Milwaukee. Chicago is overwhelming. It's a start-up operation, a twenty-four-hour Chicago news station and they need to hire a lot of people cheaply and make them work shifts that would put child-labor laws to shame. They're banking on the fact that, well, it's Chicago. The news director shows us around a very unimpressive newsroom and sits separately with each of us. He has a gold ring with his initials, MJ, on it and he keeps twisting the ring around as he tells me, "I'm a chemist. I need to put all of the parts together to make the right product." He sits back in his chair, his middle-aged belly spilling over his belt, still twisting the ring. "I'm not sure if you're right or not."

Apparently I don't fit into the test tube because he offers Paul a job but not me. Paul turns it down; the money is ridiculously low for us to be bringing in one income, and we're actually relieved. We can't wait to get back to Wisconsin. We know we're not ready for the pace of Chicago.

But Minneapolis is another story. Paul grew up in south Minneapolis, and a chance to be near his thirteen brothers and sisters (yes, thirteen) might be too hard to pass up. We apply at a local affiliate, but we agree we don't like the way they treat us during our interviews, talking down and making a really low-ball offer.

"Do you have your steady-cam license?" they ask Paul. The guy is three years out of college. He's not shooting scenes in a movie. No, he does not. This strikes us as so funny we will use it as a one-liner for

Paul and I were already engaged at my college graduation.

years, saying to each other, "Do you have your steady-cam license?" at oddball times of the day.

And again, they're counting on young journalists just wanting to be in Minneapolis. No thanks. Milwaukee feels right. We know a number of the people there because WISC and WTMJ are sister stations and share video. WTMJ is expanding its offerings, adding 4:00 and 4:30 newscasts, and they need people. We're both hired. I will be one of the new faces to replace the veteran and highly respected sportscaster Hank Stoddard, who is retiring. I know it will take a lot of convincing for some viewers in the market to accept anyone in Hank's shoes, and I am facing a mix of people at the station who are firmly in my corner and those who are gun-shy about hiring a woman. The news director says I have to be part-time news and part-time sports, the idea being to ease me into the consciousness of the people. Heaven forbid they should see a woman doing sports on a regular basis. Maybe once or twice a week they can swallow it.

On my first day, I'm in news. I'm sent to a court case. I call the Waukesha County Courthouse to find out what room to go to.

"Is it a probate case?" the receptionist asks me. Huh? I've never heard of probate. Don't even know what the word means. I just mastered linebackers and figured out what a halfback option pass was. I feel out of my element.

"I'm . . . not . . . sure." I try to say it calmly, like I clearly understand probate but simply don't know if this case is one or not.

"OK, let's look it up," she says. I am overcome with relief. I did not sound like a total idiot on my first phone call. I only felt like one. I immediately hit the dictionary and find out *probate* means a case involving a will.

They switch me to mainly feature stories for my news duties and I have to do a piece on preschoolers learning traffic rules with the help of some friendly police officers and a "safety town" with stop signs and crosswalks. Sweet, but not what I want to be doing.

Thankfully, after a few months of juggling news and sports, it's determined that, indeed, Milwaukee is ready to try a full-time female sports reporter. I'm taken off news assignments and head happily into the best job I could have ever hoped for: sportscaster. In my first few months of working sports I cover Indy car racing, beach volleyball, sailing, rugby, and the usual array of football, basketball, and baseball. I'm loving it. Each day is different and I thrive on all of the creativity. We have to write, produce, and sometimes edit our own pieces.

There are not many negatives to the job in my mind at this point, except that I occasionally get letters stamped "Sent from the Wisconsin Prison System," from a few different men, which freaks me out. I also get asked out by very sincere and honest guys who send me their pictures and bios. I write back and say I'm married.

In addition to being a woman I am a minority, and I'm not blind to the fact that this is also something some people might have to get used to. Yet, the only time I remember anyone mentioning race in my professional career was when I covered a local soccer team and that coach said during the interview, "We play the Latin style of soccer. But you know all about that, don't you?" with a laugh. Come again? I knew nothing about Latin soccer and didn't need him implying that I did.

Thankfully, most people seem to find it interesting that a Hispanic, Jewish woman is on the air reporting sports. In fact, Dennis Krause, my new sports director, tells me I have to learn to decline the many requests from people who are suddenly asking me to emcee banquets or speak to their classes.

"Say no to some of these things," he advises.

I'm feeling stretched to the limit by doing too much.

"But I don't want anyone to be mad at me."

"Who cares? You have to say no."

I'm twenty-four, still just figuring out all of this stuff. But one thing I know is that I'm content working at the local level. ESPN calls me once, early in my career, and asks if I'm still under contract. I am and I tell them that and say thank you very much for inquiring, but secretly I'm relieved I don't have to deal with the pressure of ESPN or any other network. I don't want to have to move to Connecticut and I also know in my heart of hearts that I'm not ready for ESPN, not polished enough to swim with the sharks. At the time I was friendly with a female Green Bay reporter who worked at ESPN for a while and she told me, over lunch in the Lambeau Field pressroom, how stressful it was to have to be an expert on this team one day and that team the next. She was flying all over the country and cramming on the plane just so she'd have something moderately intelligent to say when she landed and had to interview people and be live on the air.

"I feel like everything I say is so surfacy. I hardly ever get to go deeper into any one team. It's tough," she tells me. A few years later she would leave ESPN.

I stay put in Milwaukee. I love covering the teams I know. I love Wisconsin, with its camping and hiking, and we live by the shores of Lake Michigan. The state has everything I ever wanted and I feel comfortable and happy. Sixteen years later I will be heading off to cover my third Super Bowl.

SUPER BOWL XLV
FEBRUARY 2011

I SKYPE THE KIDS as soon as we land in Denver. And I mean the moment we touch down. They're just getting up in Wisconsin, while I've already watched the sun rise over two time zones. I'm stuck in the back row of the plane as I turn on the computer. The technology actually works!

"Let us see who you're sitting next to," they say over bowls of cereal. I tilt the laptop toward the portly guy next to me. Luckily he plays along, waving at strangers in pajamas halfway across the country. Then I catch a glimpse of myself in the Skype camera. I look awful: a blue baseball cap on unwashed hair, my eyes puffy and red with lack of sleep. I shudder and look away, now turning the laptop toward the skyline.

"Look guys, mountains!" That's a novelty we don't have in Wisconsin.

Three hours later I'm up and away from those mountains and landing in the strange, foreign land of Dallas. It is not my first time there. I have covered a few other games during the Holmgren years. But being here always makes me shake my head at the differences from the north. Cowboy hats and Southern drawls, well-groomed women and rancher men. Our photographer, Michael Greene, picks me up at the airport. Everyone else came out a day earlier. I had to tape a *Mike McCarthy*

Show in Green Bay and was then put on that ungodly early flight, but Michael cracks me up and I start to brighten upon landing. The sun is shining. It's warm by Wisconsin standards. Michael has a terrible sense of direction and gets us lost just trying to retrace his steps from the airport to the hotel, even with a GPS. "Recalculating," the little woman in the GPS keeps telling us. Michael calls his friend, Kenny, who lives in Dallas.

"Can you help a brother out? Do they not have street signs in this backward joint you call Dallas?" He will call Kenny at least fifteen more times that week, causing me to laugh as each request becomes more urgent and humorous.

We just have time for me to check into the mammoth media hotel, shower, and be back on the road for our first assignment. The lobby is already filled with foreign journalists, a group speaking rapid-fire Spanish in line in front of me. I marvel at the wonder of the Super Bowl. Journalists from every corner of the globe will spend two weeks analyzing all aspects of the game, every possible scenario that could happen in sixty minutes of football, and then ... whatever happens will happen. It's a little comical to me, but I am part of the machine.

The first sign of trouble occurs less than five minutes after checking in. My key card will not open the door to my room. I try it this way and that, call the front desk, and proceed to wait nearly half an hour, sitting on my suitcase, using up valuable shower time, until they send someone from maintenance. This key-card reader will give me problems all week.

I brought one pair of open-toe sandals, hoping to be able to wear them after enduring months of a harsh, I-live-next-to-one-of-the-Great-Lakes winter. I get my wish—for about two hours. Already a chill is starting to creep in. By midweek I will be at the Walmart across from Cowboys Stadium, buying industrial-strength rubber boots, the thickest socks I can find, and extra gloves. Isn't the only perk of coming south to a game like this a little warmth? Mother Nature has some cruel tricks for us. It sleets, it snows. The roads get a thick layer of ice.

"Everybody grab that salt shaker off your kitchen table and let's help out all of these out-of-town guests," a local radio station jokes. There are no salt trucks. We endure one white-knuckle drive after another, usually at 11:30 p.m., when we're all exhausted. I've never been on roads this bad in twenty-five years of steering through the upper Midwest. Some Dallas drivers literally stop in the middle of the highway, they are that paralyzed with indecision. A few look at us and shrug as we inch slowly past them, their body language saying, "Oh, well, I guess I'll just sit here for a while." Others are on their cell phones, probably telling loved ones that they are stuck on a sheet of ice.

One night I'm in the satellite truck with our engineer, Kevin Frahm. He tries to get to the on-ramp and we go sliding.

"Kevin!" I shout, grabbing the dashboard.

"I got it, I got it," he responds matter-of-factly. He's the calm sort.

"Are we having any fun down here?" I ask him.

"Are you kidding? You know we don't have fun on these trips. Everybody else has fun. But not us. This is work." And he's right. Packers fans are drinking and partying and laughing. It's clearly a blast and I wish desperately I could join in, but I can only observe the hilarity while the occasional beer gets spilled on me.

I sigh.

"I miss my kids," I tell Kevin. He's a father of three. He gets it.

"I know, I know," he says. "Hang in there."

The first night, Michael and I go to Cowboys Stadium and interview people stopping their cars in the Walmart parking lot across the way to get pictures of the dark stadium. At least the side of the building is lit up by giant portraits of some of the key Packers and Steelers players. There is also a crowd around a glamorous-looking woman speaking Spanish and I realize it's a journalist from TV Azteca who gained fame just a few months prior when she dressed provocatively at a Jets practice and was catcalled by some players. I had actually written a column about it for *Packer Plus*, a weekly newspaper. She's definitely working it here, too: dressed in tight clothes and impossibly high heels, laughing and signing autograph after autograph for a mostly male audience. We shoot our story with me in jeans and a fleece coat. I'm feeling inferior next to her, yet much more comfortable. Michael and I head back to the hotel around 10 p.m. and I think to myself: you've slept just two hours of the past thirty-eight. I shake my head and collapse under the acres of white sheets.

For my first full day I've been assigned to the Steelers. I need to wait for their plane to come in before scampering to the hotel for interviews. First, we are taken to the holding area inside an airplane hangar where a jumbo jet is parked just above our heads, its nose peeking down at us as we wait for the team plane. There are tables of bagels and cream cheese and bowls of fruit out for the media. Many are playing cards or reading the paper. A couple of times we have a false alarm when someone says a plane is coming and we all run outside only to discover it's someone else. Finally, we're given the real five-minute warning. Dozens of reporters stand on risers sipping coffee in the chilly sunshine. The NFL Network is next to me, doing very serious commentary on the plane arriving.

"Here it comes, just a few minutes late."

The Steelers are the big, bad boys of this game. They've already won two Super Bowls in recent years. Their quarterback is a veteran. Their star wide receiver, Hines Ward, comes off the plane fully decked in cowboy gear.

"Just having a little fun," he'll say later. But I realize the Steelers are not nearly as motivated as the Packers. They are searching for ways to motivate themselves. Many players announce they're dedicating this Super Bowl to Flozell Adams, who recently joined them from the Cowboys and has never won a ring. They remind me of the Los Angeles Lakers in their heyday. I remember Phil Jackson wanting to get a ring for his assistant, Frank Hamblen. Same concept. A victory would just be gravy to many of the Steelers. The Packers are going to win this damn thing, I think to myself. They really are.

Yet I also notice Coach McCarthy looks a little wide-eyed upon walking into his opening press conference. He has never been to a Super Bowl before, not even as a fan or an assistant coach, a fact that stunned me. Don't all coaches come here just to network at some point? He walks into the grand ballroom at the Packers hotel and sizes up the media contingent—which is at least six times bigger than anything he's used to in Green Bay—and he looks nervous. The only thing that will bite these Packers, we all decide, is a severe case of the jitters.

Day two is media day and the weather is downright terrible: freezing rain. We all pile into media buses that crawl the forty-five minutes it takes to get to the stadium, water pelting the windows with little clicks. I have to chuckle when I see some of the women still wearing stilettos and sparkly cocktail dresses, slipping on the accumulating ice as they run from the bus to the check-in area, umbrellas protesting in the wind. Some people look at media day as their chance to shine. The place is crawling with serious journalists and jokesters: Letterman and Leno have sent their people, Comedy Central, too. The highlight of my day is seeing one of my kids' heroes, Jeff from Nickelodeon's *BrainSurge*, who is wearing full superhero garb: tights, a cape, and a mask. In an hour's time we have to gather as many interviews as possible, using ladders and elbowing each other to get good spots. To make sure we don't double up on interviews, the other sports anchors from my station and I have divided up whom we're going to get.

The stadium towers over all of us like a cruise ship over fish. It's the largest domed stadium in the world. It holds 80,000 fans—about 7,000 more than Lambeau Field, but it feels even bigger than that. I stand in awe of its grotesque size, thinking about the ostentatious amount of money spent on its creation. This is, after all, Jerry's World. That's Jerry Jones—the billionaire owner of the Dallas Cowboys. I feel the vast emptiness coming from the top rafters. The floor is choked with reporters and players in their crisply washed uniforms, but we take up only one one-thousandth of the space. The stadium is a beast. A quiet and dormant beast but one that could crush nearby apartments if it decided to take a walk. It could send sound waves to Oklahoma if it decided to scream.

"Take a look around and tell me what you think," I say to running back Brandon Jackson, one of the Packers I've been assigned to cover.

"Oh, man. It's an amazing stadium," he says, his hands in the collar of his green and gold jersey, his eyes scanning the massive roof and then the Jumbotron, which is notorious for being Texas-large to match its landlord. "That's probably the size of my house."

Safety Nick Collins gets his own little "booth" to conduct interviews, while the lesser-known athletes on the team have to stand. Collins leans forward into the mass of microphones and reflects on the fact that he is a Super Bowl player. "I made it, I made it. It's a dream come true," he says. "It's been a blessing, it's been a long journey. I've been chasing this

The insanity that is Super Bowl media day, less than one week before Super Bowl XLV at Cowboys Stadium. I was somewhere in the middle.
COURTESY OF ROD BURKS

journey for six years now. I have the chance to make it very special and hopefully I can do that."

A well-known player-turned-broadcaster is one of the mass of reporters asking questions in another area. He says to Greg Jennings, "Tell me, man, what does it feel like to be in a Super Bowl? Tell me."

"It's the greatest," says Jennings. "I wish everyone could experience this." It dawns on me how many players go their whole careers without a shot at the big game.

We find the Packers general manager, Ted Thompson, off to the side, only a few print reporters around him.

"You must be so proud to bring your team here," I begin.

He tells me that they're not done yet, to talk to him Sunday night. He repeats that theme as he answers another reporter's question: "We're happy to be here, but we're not all giddy. We can do the giddy part later."

You can tell he's tight. He measures his words even more carefully than usual. It's clear that it's not enough to just make the big game; you have to win it or nobody remembers you.

Ted is from Atlanta, Texas, a tiny town a few hours from Dallas. I had the idea a few weeks before to go and do a story on his hometown. I started by calling the only high school.

"Good morning, Atlanta High School," said the receptionist in the thickest Southern drawl I had ever heard. "May I help you?"

I explained the situation and she said, "I think a few people in town might still know Ted." She gave me the number of a local guy and I thanked her and hung up. When I spoke to Ted's former high school classmate he seemed friendly and willing to do the story, but as the week leading up to my flying down there went along, he stopped returning my calls for some unknown reason. I still was willing to make the two-hour drive to Atlanta and stop in at a coffee shop, asking the locals how they felt about one of their own being the GM of the Packers, but it didn't happen for me. Because of flights and schedules set up for other stories, I couldn't be spared to spend the whole day chasing down this story. I reluctantly handed it off to one of our news anchors, who was going to arrive the day before me and would have time.

As it turned out, our anchor called it one of the least rewarding stories he had been a part of. The drive was closer to three hours—each way—and the town itself was even smaller than any of us had imagined. The news anchor had a hard time finding anyone who remembered Ted. The friend whose number we had, never called him back either. Sometimes that will happen when you're trying to set up a story: people will change their minds, or stop calling.

"Total waste of time" was our anchor's summation, although he did get enough material, barely, to put together a minute-long piece.

Our station has a trailer in the media compound. It's just about as dull as you can get. Imagine one of those golf-scoring trailers minus the fancy water and snacks and you just about have it: plain white walls, long tables, a few phones, and some computers—bare as can be with a couple of tiny windows, and a Porta-Potty for a bathroom. It's here that we spend at least six hours of every day for the next eight days, inputting script information and editing. Then we walk the fifty feet out the back door and climb a rickety riser to join dozens of other television stations using the stadium as a backdrop. One night it rains so hard all of my notes get soaked despite an umbrella. I am squinting to try to see

Spending time with WTMJ coworkers Rod Burks, Michael Greene, and Rick Rietbrock right after the media-day crowd dispersed. COURTESY OF ROD BURKS

what comes next in my segment. As soon as the show ends I ball up the notes and heave them over the edge of the railing in a dramatic show of disgust. Then I retrieve them and find a garbage can. I can't litter, even here, where the only constants are the humming of electricity and a never-ending smell of exhaust.

I Skype the kids again from inside the trailer, showing them everything and everybody. All of the reporters and photographers know them by name and wave cheerily. The kids hold up their homework and tell me about a band concert I'll be missing. They are pumped about the Packers, though, and I am, too. There's no question that, aside from being homesick, it is exciting to be at an event of this magnitude.

Days three, four, and five blend into one another. There is always an 8:00 a.m. press conference, and it's always at the Packers team hotel, which is no less than one hour from ours with morning traffic. We take turns doing the early shift so we can all sleep in once or twice and get to the hotel exercise room every now and again. The day I have the 8:00 a.m., I am bleary-eyed from going to sleep after 1:00 and meeting in the lobby at 7:00. We grab breakfast at a Burger King drive-thru and barely make it in time to set up. Truly, there are too many interview opportunities, and after a while there is practically nothing left to ask. We are grasping and so is everyone else. We start having players interview each other. We are in possession of tons of footage, too much to log. A lot of it goes by the wayside. "Just give me the gold" is our mantra. The rest is on the proverbial cutting-room floor.

One night I am told I have to be live from Fort Worth. There's a big, open-air plaza there that is supposed to be filled with fans and should make for good visuals. If you've never been to Fort Worth, just know this: the airport code DFW is a misnomer. Fort Worth is a major haul from Dallas. Michael gets us turned around again—surprise—and we're racing to make it on time. By the time we get to downtown, Fort Worth traffic is crawling.

We switch drivers and I drop Michael at the live shot location so he can shoot our main news anchor at the top of the 5:00 newscast. Now I have to find parking. I'm sweating as I look at my watch and know I'm on in less than

Writing and editing in our second home—the "golf trailer" outside Cowboys Stadium. COURTESY OF ROD BURKS

fifteen minutes and the line of cars around me isn't moving. Suddenly I see a restaurant with valet parking. There's nothing a little extra tip won't get you in this world and I literally run the two blocks back to the plaza.

Now comes another problem. The open-air plaza is a great idea *if* the weather is good. But it's butt-kicking cold. Some college-age girls are handing out hot chocolate near the ESPN stage, trying to get people to watch a live broadcast. But mostly the place is deserted. We resort to showing the giant, lit-up map of Texas in the plaza instead of the hordes of people we'd envisioned happily milling around behind us. In between live shots I have to go into a Western-wear store and stamp my feet around just to stop my toes from becoming frostbitten—and this is with my industrial Walmart boots and two pairs of socks!

I'm feeling like the last thing I need is a dose of criticism, but the only phone call I get from the station is a manager yelling at me for saying *ESPN* on our air.

"It's like telling people to turn the channel," he says, exasperated. Apparently I wasn't supposed to explain what the giant stage and few people in the plaza were there for. I walk away annoyed, my hot chocolate long since cold.

By now one of our photographers is sick and another is on the verge of being sent home due to a slipped disc in his back. We're all feeling on edge. I have to mediate a tiff between two photographers, each of whom thinks the other is getting a shorter shift that day. Then it's time to edit for the 10 p.m. broadcast. Because other people from our station are in the warm satellite truck, I am stuck with the laptop and I need to find a place to work. I proceed to spend the next two hours alone in a booth at Qdoba, nibbling on a veggie burrito and trying to edit enough video for two hits on the 10 p.m., plus our extra twenty-minute special. This is the glamorous life, I think to myself, my feet still numb.

There are some really enjoyable parts to covering a Super Bowl, but the best is actually designed for the mountain of radio stations in attendance. It's called Radio Row and takes up the entire first-floor convention space of the hotel. You descend the escalator into organized chaos. Each station has its own table and there are *hundreds* of stations, small and large, the vast majority from markets that have no connection to the Packers or Steelers. Markets like Boston, which can simply afford to send people and think it will be cool for their listeners to know that, damn it, they were there, at Super Bowl XLV. The stations and their tables cover the base of the floor, wires and cables everywhere, snaking to outlets. There is a constant hum of conversation punctuated by laughter, mostly male voices in the entire space.

Around the rim of the room are booths. You've got people from major companies showing off their products, one small food area that's always crowded with those looking for free samples, and reps from next year's

Super Bowl in Indianapolis handing out swag. I grab an orange knit hat and a pin for my kids. But it's what else is happening in the room that is truly interesting. Celebrities, celebrities, and, wow, another celebrity. Most are of the football variety. John Elway is here and Michael Irvin. Irvin played against the Packers for years as a wide receiver for Dallas. He gives us a funny interview talking about *The Wizard of Oz* and somehow relating it to the Packers. I ask him two short questions and he spends four minutes in a rambling, train-of-thought answer, part of it includes:

"[Aaron Rodgers] is real cool, calm, and sneakily shy. I'm a man and it's attractive the way he plays. It really is. I'm so sick of Pittsburgh, they've got six [titles] already and the Cowboys only have five. I need the Packers [to win]. I love them and I need them. I want you to be like the wizard and tap your toes three times on *The Wizard of Oz*. Make the trophy say 'There's no place like home.' And take it home. Let it go see Vince Lombardi, take it home. Take Vince Lombardi home at least for this year."

Irvin says all of this with hand gestures and facial expressions that photographer Michael and I enjoy immensely.

Then there are the movie stars, Hugh Jackman and Adam Sandler, and the supermodels, Brooklyn Decker and Marisa Miller. Even Miss America is there. Some people are desperate to be interviewed. One interviewee talks to us for a long time, but can't remember the quarterback's full name.

"Rodgers, right?"

"Yes . . . do you know his first name?" I ask her.

"Umm . . . I forget."

Up-and-coming country singers are wandering around with guitars, hoping to get some exposure. But the really big fish, you almost can't touch. They all have their handlers with clipboards in hand, checking their watches and acting busy at all moments.

"Just a second, I'm on with New York," they'll say, leaning deeper into their Bluetooths. Elway's handler tells me I may ask him one question in between radio interviews. One question only. And he makes it clear that they're doing us a big favor. I ponder the best way to get the most out of him in one query, finally coming up with, "What are your overall impressions of the Packers organization—both back in the day when you beat them in Super Bowl XXXII and now that they're finally back in it? Impressions of Ted Thompson, the team, everything, what do you think?" It's a ridiculously bloated question, but he gives a long answer and I'm pleased. I can cut that up into at least two sound bites, maybe three.

We talk to Caleb Hanie, the Bears backup quarterback who took over for an injured Jay Cutler in the NFC championship game and put up a good fight before the Packers finally won.

"It could have been us," Hanie says, sighing regretfully as his eyes sweep the room.

I see former Packer Antonio Freeman, who won a Super Bowl with the Packers in 1997. He says he feels like he's in a time warp. He's the perfect person to offer advice to this current Packers team.

"It doesn't last forever. I thought it was forever. I thought we'd get back again before my career ended and I never got back to it," he says. "Cherish the moment, pay attention to details because it's not about who the best team was this year—it's about who executes the best and who makes the least mistakes on Sunday. It's a small window, it's sixty minutes but it will determine for the rest of the year who the best team is this year."

I'm allowed to interview two supermodels as they walk from one table to another. One of them does the interview with her hairstylist behind her, fluffing and spraying the whole time. But I find the women themselves genuine. They know football and give thoughtful answers about who might win and why. Decker is married to tennis player Andy Roddick, and as luck would have it we know that he recently tweeted that he was at Lambeau Field with his father. She talks fondly and with affection about her father-in-law's love of the Packers. The women are beautiful, but I think they would be even more so without the heavy makeup.

Adam Sandler's handler won't be bothered by a petty little TV station from Milwaukee.

"We are booked, just completely booked. We have no time, honey," he says, showing me the clipboard for evidence. I spy some open areas in his fancy, color-coded calendar, but he shoots me down.

"No, we're running late so that turns into that and that into that. There's just no way."

"I could hang around just in case," I say. "But if I'm just going to annoy you and waste both of our time, tell me now."

"If you hang around, I will deny you out of spite." OK, I get it. They're booked, just completely booked, honey. I manage to stick a microphone on the table when Sandler is being interviewed by WTMJ radio, but the audio is not good and I move on.

My favorite interview in Radio Row (aside from the rambling Michael Irvin) is Jay Mohr, an actor/comedian who was the bad-guy agent from *Jerry Maguire*. We're standing in a scene much like the one where Tom Cruise's and Cuba Gooding Jr.'s characters have to "walk the lobby." We talk some football. He's a Jets fan and bemoans the fact that the Packers beat his team earlier in the season.

"Your kicker—who is it? Crosby? We made him a Hall-of-Famer that day," Mohr says in his New York accent, which he covers well in movies.

I ask Mohr if he can deliver a line from *Jerry Maguire*, and he switches right into character, looking at the camera directly and saying, "I came here to fire you, Jerry. You know what I went through knowing I was going to have to fire my mentor? Carrying that around in my head for a week? Could you get past yourself for a second?" I thank him, grateful that Mohr has time for little old Milwaukee.

The next day the station decides we need a Super Bowl story targeted toward our demo. This is slang for demographic, and in this case, in layman's terms, it truly means women who control where their household income is spent and have command of the remote. We need something that has nothing to do with Xs and Os. Our demo woman doesn't want that. She wants, she wants . . . well, what does she want? We spend about thirty minutes on a conference call pitching ideas and trying to decide what she would be clamoring to see. Finally it's decided that I will put together a piece using all of the supermodels, actors, and wannabe country singers we have. I'm looking forward to the piece until an editing disaster strikes.

We have the satellite truck parked outside of a bar that's supposed to be *the* hangout for Packers fans. Our cable runs across the icy parking lot through the back door to a camera set up in what I can only describe as a mosh pit of green and gold. I have to do live shots from here with Mike Jacobs, the news anchor, all through the early evening, scarfing down a grilled cheese in between shows and using the table of a nice older couple to hold my plate while we stand next to them. The place is getting so crowded, it has that too-many-people smell. Things are spilling everywhere. Music is blaring and waiters are trying to make their way through the crowd with trays of drinks held high above their heads.

When we finally get done with the early shows, I have yet to start editing the long piece for the 10 p.m. newscast. My heart is beating since I know this will not be easy. The editing machine has been acting up and no one is around to help. The rest of our crew has gone back to the media compound. Ira, Mike's photographer, needs to go with him to shoot and edit another story. This one's on me. It's going along OK, until it isn't. I'm not savvy enough on the system to figure out the problem, so I'm on the phone with Rick Rietbrock, the producer at the compound, and I finally have to have Ira rescue the situation.

We're trying to feed what has been this heavily promoted story and it won't feed and it's scaring the crap out of me. I can visualize the producers pacing back in Milwaukee. Ira is madly pulling cables from one machine to another, rebooting something else, and cursing under his breath. This ain't good, I'm thinking. We miss our first "slot" (the time it was supposed to air) and our second slot. Now the piece is being bumped to the twenty-minute special. Milwaukee says they got it, but not all of it. They will need to do a few edits and make it work. An interview with comedian Frank Caliendo, a Wisconsin native who does spot-on impersonations, won't be in the final cut. I'm bummed. Something I tried so hard to deliver will air late and be incomplete. I force a smile on TV, but my heart sinks.

A few days before the game, things start to break down in the hotel. The hot water in the shower comes when it wants to. The power being pulled from all of those laptops and radio stations overwhelms the system and there is a partial blackout. Hallway lights are dimmed and then, the coup de grâce, the bank of elevators to my tower stops working. At first I don't realize this and I wait almost twenty minutes, pushing the down button over and over. Finally I call the front desk.

"Oh, so sorry," they say. "If you need to get down right now, you'll have to walk."

I do have to get down right now, but I'm on the twenty-seventh floor with two heavy editing laptops and a backpack laden with microphones. I find the fire exit and start walking. And walking. A woman is huffing and puffing heading up the other direction. At least I'm going down, but I'm still pretty winded when I get to the bottom and emerge out the emergency side door onto the street. Another glamorous Super Bowl moment.

As the week draws to a close I'm feeling really tired. Sixteen-hour days eventually catch up with you. One day, fellow reporter Lance Allan is driving and I simply can't wake up my brain. Usually ten minutes of shutting my eyes and a Diet Coke will recharge the batteries enough to keep going, but this time I feel like my whole being is protesting. It scares me how tired I am. I would like to not have to take an Ambien every night, but I can't come down quickly without it. I feel my well-being slipping.

Soon enough it's game day and the excitement level is back up around Dallas, despite my fatigue. The hotel provides a media breakfast that could have fed thousands more people. I wonder at the waste of food. There are omelet stations, salad bars, racks of meat, pastries, oatmeal, anything you want. I try to fuel up, knowing it will be a long day. It's sunny and finally back to a tinge of warmth (just in time for all of us to leave the next day). We stand outside the media compound (remember—white trailer) and watch the crazies go by. Doing a story here is a piece of cake: there's Elvis, a whole group in different president masks, an older couple who announce that they drove all night just to be a part of the scene. The streets around the stadium are clogged with hawkers selling items and even stilt walkers. It's like a carnival, and almost all of them want to be on TV.

"Hey, interview me!" they yell.

We have to do a 5:00 newscast that no one will watch because the game kicks off at 5:40 and they're already watching the pregame show on FOX. We fill the show and the three of us on-air people—Lance Allan, Rod Burks, and me—run to the stadium. The security check-in will take a while: put your bags down for the dogs to sniff, come this way to be wanded, go through this metal detector, sign this waiver, that waiver, get your bags back, get the proper tag for the bag, show ID, and finally be let through.

We get to our seats right before kickoff. They're handing out boxed lunches and little radio earpieces to listen to the game. The media overflow is so great, we are actually in the stands, in a makeshift media area with some sort of long table in front of us. The legroom is nonexistent, but at least we have seats. I can see the area across the field where controversy has blown up. The seats were deemed unsafe and hundreds were left outside holding tickets with no place to sit. They are fuming mad. It will be a national story the NFL will be trying to move past for a year.

The game itself flies by. A Nick Collins interception; Jordy Nelson puts in a big performance. The Packers look good. At halftime we all stay in our seats to catch the Black Eyed Peas. What resembles a sea of ants moves the stage on and off the field in record time and Fergie descends from the ceiling. My older son loves the "Peas," while I basically know one or two songs.

With fellow sports anchors Rod Burks and Lance Allan, crammed into our seats for Super Bowl XLV. COURTESY OF ROD BURKS

The scene just after the Black Eyed Peas performed at halftime of Super Bowl XLV. I would be leaving soon to walk through the rain with my staticky radio. COURTESY OF ROD BURKS

My job is to be outside the stadium when the game ends. I need to do this because the station managers want us, the NBC station, to go live when this FOX game is over, and FOX owns rights to the inside action. How many people will switch channels at that point is never made clear, but I need to be there, back on the rickety riser and ready to rehash the game. To do this I must leave shortly after the third quarter, just as the Steelers are making things interesting. OK, I think. I have this handy, dandy radio. I shall listen to the rest on the long walk back to the compound. Nice plan. Didn't work. The radio apparently only functions inside the stadium, so with every step farther away I'm hearing "Greg Jennings . . . static, static, horrible buzz, static, static . . . great play!" I have to chuckle. I may be the only football fan in the world who has no idea what's going on and I'm less than a parking lot away from Greg Jennings. Plus, the clueless person is the one who is supposed to talk expertly about what she just saw? To make matters worse it starts to rain. I call our producer and ask, "What just happened? My radio died."

"They're going to win, they're going to win!" The joy in his voice is overflowing. He's been a Packers fan his whole life. I am thrilled for the

Packers and for the state of Wisconsin, but I'm also wet and I have to get into place for a live shot. Michael meets me there, bundled head to toe in rain gear. WTMJ comes to me when the game ends and we show what's happening around us, which is to say a bunch of dejected Steelers fans filing out. The Packers fans are still inside where my colleagues are and they're getting the best stuff: Charles Woodson crying, Aaron Rodgers pumping his fist. I have to stand in the rain for another hour before they announce that I'm clear.

Now that the game is over, I have a little problem. The station wants me to be back on the air at the stadium at 6:00 a.m. the next day for the early morning show. I've been going around and around with one of the managers for days. His point: We send you to Dallas. We want presence. My point: I can do it on tape. Otherwise, I will get less than two hours of sleep and have to drive an hour each way in the middle of the night in an unfamiliar area after working one of the most intense days of my career. I already have a sore throat, too. Not good enough for him. We are at a stalemate. I put my foot down. If you want me to do it, book me into a hotel near the stadium so I can take out the driving part. No, he says. Then I'm sorry, I can't and won't do it, I tell him. It's the first time I can recall saying no to anything at the station. He backs off. Lance looks at me. "Wow, you really told them."

"Honestly, Lance, if they fired me over that I wouldn't be that upset. We're working our tails off, but I will draw the line at jeopardizing our health." I never speak of it again with management.

Back in Wisconsin the kids are going crazy at a Super Bowl party put on by some friends. Paul e-mails me pictures of them jumping around in their green and gold shirts, high-fiving and screaming right after the final kneel-down. I can't believe the Packers did it. I'm ecstatic for them.

The hotel lobby bar is less crowded than it's been all week. As usual I've had next to nothing to eat since the big breakfast. So I go into the bar with my friend Lori Nickel, who covers the Packers for the *Milwaukee Journal Sentinel*. We've seen each other about twice in passing all week, despite covering many of the same events. We swap stories over tortilla chips and artichoke dip and I find out why it's so quiet in the bar. Many reporters, Lori included, are on the first available flight out of town. That means middle-of-the-night getaways or, like Lori, first thing in the morning. Lori tells me she plans not to sleep at all (it's already 2:00 a.m.), to be at the airport by 5:00 a.m., home by 9:00, and then to crawl into bed all day while her kids are at school.

I'm jealous. I won't get home until Monday night. I think of the players and coaches. How happy they must be. They'll sleep well tonight. The journalists? Not so much. This is Lori's first Super Bowl and she was shocked by the amount of work it was. It's different for print reporters, though. She can write in her hotel room. She doesn't have to be live at 10:00 p.m. from some faraway locale. Still, she says she was constantly blogging and turning out three to four stories per day. We agree that a Super Bowl is a monstrous amount of work. I finally go to bed for my last night in Dallas.

When I wake up, my first thought is that Lori is already home. Damn. I have to fill a lot of time until a late-afternoon flight. For the first time all week I go for a run outside. Now I'm finally getting to see some nice parts of Dallas. There's a park and an interesting-looking art museum. We're not far from the grassy knoll and I make our producer Rick go there with me and take some pictures. I'd love to go up into the museum, but the line snakes around the block, most people still in their Packers or Steelers gear, obviously trying to get in a little tourism before they go home, too.

At the Dallas airport I load up on Super Bowl XLV gear to give to all of the friends who helped out. It's overpriced, but I feel I need to repay them some way. I get hats, stickers, magnets, footballs, and a fleece pullover for Julianne, who did the overnight duty.

Rick and I have to fly through Louisville this time. There's enough of a layover for dinner, but the only restaurant in the airport is just past the security checkpoint. It's not until we're trying to get back through to the gate that I realize I can't find my boarding pass for the second flight. Rick has his and goes through. Time is ticking. Oh, dear God, please don't let me get stuck in Louisville tonight. I feel a magnetic pull toward my kids. The security guy calls the American Airlines desk.

"If you run, they'll print a new one," he says. I've never run so fast in my life. I get back to the plane seconds before they shut the door and close my eyes in relief.

My older son is up when I finally walk in the door.

"Hi," he says, rising up off the couch. A big smile spreads across his face and he comes right over for a hug.

"Hi, sweetie, I missed you." I tousle his hair, trying to sneak in a few kisses while he ducks me, but I can see he's beaming.

The younger one is already asleep. I simply can't resist crawling into bed with him and kissing his soft head a few times. He stirs.

"Mommy, is that you? Is it really you? Are you home?" he mumbles.

"Yes, honey, it's me." I inhale the smell of his head. I made it. I was not felled by airplane crashes, terrorism, or icy roads. I survived eight days.

"You're really home? Will you sleep with me tonight?" he asks.

"Of course I will," I say and wrap my arms around him.

The next day I am bone-tired—my first day off in almost three weeks. The Packers are having a welcome-home celebration at Lambeau Field, but I am thankful we have other people covering it. Plus, I had signed up long ago to help at the elementary school book fair. Now I feel too spent to do even that. I e-mail the woman in charge.

"No problem," she writes back. "Unless you have a burning desire for some book fair mojo, you're fine. Stay home."

I stay home.

SUPER BOWL XXXI
JANUARY 1997

EARLIER IN MY CAREER I had the honor of covering two other Super Bowls. Before that, the Packers had not been to the big game since the Vince Lombardi days, enduring year after year of down seasons. So when Ron Wolf, Reggie White, Brett Favre, and Mike Holmgren came along, it was a sight to behold.

There is a picture of Holmgren from Super Bowl XXXI forever burned into my mind. It was taken by Pepper Burruss, the Packers head athletic trainer who has documented more behind-the-scenes Packers history through his camera hobby than anyone else, save the official team photographers.

The thing that makes it so startling is that Holmgren is lying flat on his back, his head propped on some towels and feet up on a chair. It is less than half an hour before kickoff. He is studying his play sheet. It's such a real, human picture of a football coach, the kind you almost never see. Pepper will tell the story of how he got it several times over the years.

"The door was ever so slightly ajar. I tapped on the door and saw coach in there, lying on his back. I didn't want to disturb him, so I just said, 'Coach, Kodak moment?' He gave me a slight nod. I snapped one photo and closed the door the way it had been."

Pepper shared this photo with us for a feature story we called "Pepper's Pics." Of everything we did in those Super Bowl years, that one photo stands out the most.

But first, we have the NFC championship game, the first one to be held at Lambeau since the Ice Bowl. The Packers are hosting the Carolina Panthers.

The weather is a typical January-in-Wisconsin day: cold but sunny. My problem is I did not sleep the night before. We were put up in a Green Bay hotel, one of those low-rent ones where people party all night. And that's exactly what happened. At about 3:00 a.m. I called the room next to mine where music was blasting and voices were booming through the thin wall.

"Vince Lombardi," the man answered with ripples of laughter behind him.

Funny. Very funny. Could they please keep it down so we could all get some sleep?

"Oh, sure," he says. But they never do. In fact, I think they turn it up to bother me. I'm miserable in the morning. It's the early game and we have to eat and get to the stadium. I feel like I slept twenty minutes. This could be one of the biggest days in Packers history and I'm walking around like a car ran over me. I drag myself through the day, grumbling under my breath the whole time about my lack of sleep, but as the game draws to a close and the Packers beat Carolina, adrenaline kicks in.

We all run onto the field. Favre is hoisting the trophy on the stage set up by the NFL. He's grinning, his braces and the trophy gleaming in the sun.

"How about that, Green Bay?" shouts Wolf to the crowd. In the locker room afterward, chaos ensues. Players are jumping around and screaming. It's not like a baseball celebration—there's no champagne—but it's close. I see Packers president and CEO Bob Harlan off to the side.

"Was there a moment, one moment, when it all hit you?" I ask. "Something you think you'll look back on?"

Harlan starts to answer, then stops. He's choked up. Now tears are coming down his face. He's telling us about standing on the sideline as the clock wound down, knowing they were going to the Super Bowl.

"I'm sorry, I'm sorry," he keeps saying, wiping tears from his eyes.

"No, no, it's OK," I answer. I'm thinking this is one of the best sound bites I've ever had. We will replay it several times that night. It's an understandable emotion he's expressing, the same one Packers fans everywhere had.

"My parents bawled like babies," my friend tells me. I forget about being tired as we go through the night, with extended coverage on the 10:00 p.m. news.

New Orleans is next. We're all excited. This is uncharted territory for any station in the state. I've never been to New Orleans and look forward to a whole different city, especially one with Bourbon Street. But we have to work like dogs before we even leave for the game. Packers hype is in overdrive. We have done stories all season on everything: the Packers' tailor, the woman who fixes rips in their uniforms after every game, the guy who washes their cars in the parking lot, the team's official priest, and one story called "Packers Pets" that gets a little dangerous when my photographer Dave is bitten by Santana Dotson's Rottweiler, Thor. I had to slam the patio door on Thor's nose to keep him from attacking all of us. Dave dripped blood from his arm. Dotson's wife, Monique, had warned us not to come outside, but Dave opened the door anyway.

"I'm not getting any natural sound. I need her to wear a microphone," he had said, approaching Monique with the black wireless microphone. Thor attacked in about two seconds and Monique started screaming. She was pregnant and I had visions flash in my mind of Thor turning on her or of all of us hiding in closets to avoid his teeth. I shuddered with relief when the door slammed in the dog's face.

But we had to go to the emergency room. I drove with Dave moaning and holding his arm. He turned a little white as I tried to steer, talk calmly to him, and not have a panic attack myself. Once at Bellin Hospital, Dave needed lots of treatment for deep puncture wounds, and Dotson had to quarantine his dog for a week to make sure it wasn't rabid. I felt bad for Dave but also sorry that we disobeyed Monique's orders. The injuries will take Dave off the Packers beat for weeks.

Meanwhile, we still need to be live every night in Green Bay. I practically move into my hotel room.

"Can we please just get one day off to do laundry?" I ask our sports director, Dennis.

"Only if you shoot enough standups to get us through tomorrow," is his answer. We need to fake that we are live in Green Bay so we can go home briefly. I get a twenty-four-hour pass and feel like I've been let out of jail when I get south of Manitowoc. It is just enough time to do a few loads of wash before I have to turn around and head back up. We're on conference calls all the time, figuring out how many people to send and when. Our news director decides to go a little nuts. We send a contingent of more than thirty people and essentially do every newscast from there. A competing station does the complete opposite. They send just a handful of people.

"Idiots," some of our managers say. "This is huge."

And they seem to be right. Everything Packers is getting monstrous ratings. We create more and more specials. The sales department is having a field day. Schools in Wisconsin are holding pep rallies and teaching kids "the Packarena," a knockoff of the then-popular Macarena. In New Orleans, we just need to find content to fill these specials.

Before the Super Bowl we contracted with a couple of players to do one-on-one interviews with us. I'm assigned Don Beebe and Antonio Freeman. When the Packers bus arrives at the hotel the very first day, I need to get Beebe a note telling him when and where to meet us for the first interview.

"Don. Don Beebe. This is for you," I yell as the players are filing through the lobby, separated from the rest of us by a red rope, the kind you'd see at a movie premiere. I walk closer to him. He leans over the rope, grabs the paper, nods, and continues on his way, but that phrase becomes a running joke between all of the reporters at our station.

"DON! DON BEEBE! . . . *This is for yoooouuu* . . . ," my coworkers will mock me time and again, sashaying across the floor. We all get a good laugh out of it. It's not the only funny moment.

One of our other sports anchors, Kevin Hunt, gets sent to Kiln, Mississippi, to do a story on Favre's hometown. He's driving back and calls, telling us the names of the people he interviewed so we can input the information onto a graphic. Our sports director doesn't hear him correctly and thinks Kevin is saying "Famous Thamous" as his first name, so that's how the name of Favre's friend appears on screen.

"I see you took the liberty of adding 'Famous' to his name," Kevin says when he sees it on the air.

"What do you mean? That's what you told me," counters Dennis.

"I did not. I said Thamous. I just had to repeat it several times because you couldn't hear me."

"How was I to know?" Dennis asks. "I just thought it was one of those Southern nickname things, like [Favre's agent] 'Bus' Cook."

Famous Thamous goes down in television history and I am on the floor laughing so hard I'm crying.

We also have a running joke going that we always say the Packers look "loose and confident" when they arrive anywhere and step off their bus.

"The Packers got to their New Orleans hotel at about 3:00 p.m. They looked loose and confident," we'll assertively report, admitting later that we truly have no idea if they are loose and confident.

"But we can't say they're tight and scared, can we?" we joke.

The opening press conference is once again in the grand ballroom, chandeliers hanging overhead and several hundred reporters and photographers crowded into the room. Holmgren strides in, cool as a cucumber, as usual. As he's talking, I notice he is wearing a ring I haven't seen on him before. Is that his Super Bowl ring from San Francisco, when he was an assistant? I'm sitting near the back of the room, so I'm squinting to try and see it. I think it is, but will I look like a jerk if I ask him about it and it's not a Super Bowl ring? I take a deep breath and raise my hand. The moderator brings the microphone to me.

"Mike, is that your Super Bowl ring?" I hold my breath for the answer, hoping he won't say, "No, that's my class ring. I've been wearing it nonstop for the past five years. Haven't you noticed?"

"Yes, it is," says Holmgren, to my relief, explaining that he put it on as a motivator for the guys. I can hear cameras zooming in to the ring as he holds it up.

"Good catch," whispers a Green Bay TV reporter next to me. I'm just glad I didn't make a fool of myself in front of so many people.

I will do several one-on-ones with Beebe and Freeman throughout the week. I sit with Beebe in the hotel's first-floor restaurant, a piece we call "Beebe's Lemonade" based on what we both drink. We also go to the hotel room where his wife, Diana, and new baby girl are staying and shoot there. The birth of this baby was a huge deal a few weeks before.

"We have to get the Beebe baby," our news director keeps saying. Whoever gets the first picture of the Beebe baby will apparently be immortalized. I had talked to his wife on the phone from her hospital bed.

"Oh, no, I look awful. You can't come over," she told me. "I'll do an interview over the phone, though." We settle for that, but it was not the Beebe baby coverage they had envisioned.

Beebe also walks through the streets of New Orleans, looking at souvenir shops with us. Then we want to see if Packers fans can recognize the baby-faced Beebe not in uniform. We buy a shirt that has pictures of Packers on it—him included—and stand outside the store, waiting for fans.

"Do you see that guy? Do you know who it is?" he asks the two women who are first to come by. He's pointing at the artist's depiction of him on the shirt.

"Umm. . . . Who is that? Nancy, do you know?" the women look at each other.

"Oh, wait, is that Don Beebe?" They are squinting at the image. It still hasn't dawned on them that the real Beebe is the one holding the shirt.

"It sure is. Handsome fella, huh?" he says and points to himself.

"*Oh, my God!* It's Don Beebe. Nancy, get the camera!" The women are beside themselves now. Beebe is a good sport, signing autographs and laughing with them.

Beebe goes back into the store and the clerk shows him a replica of the "locker room cap" the winning team will get to wear. It's black with purple, green, gold, and yellow music notes, and squiggly lines on it, very festive and New Orleans looking.

"Locker room cap," says the clerk. He has a thick Middle Eastern accent. "Take it. You will win. You will need it."

"No," says Beebe. "I'm not touching it yet. I don't want to jinx anything."

We decide to also go shopping with Freeman. He takes us to a men's clothing store he's eyed. It's filled with colorful sweaters and big leather jackets. Freeman loves it. He browses for a while, yelling out, "Can I get a hello?" when we walk through the door and then waving and pumping his fist when we leave. Then we move on to a camera store. Freeman wants to buy a camera for a family member. The guy behind the counter recognizes him immediately.

"Two touchdowns and game MVP. I guarantee it," he says to Freeman. "You'll see. I'm a little bit psychic."

Apparently his powers of looking into the future are not quite what he thinks. Desmond Howard is MVP. Freeman contributes three catches and one touchdown.

We also pass a storefront with Cheeseheads in the window.

"Do your parents own a Cheesehead?" I ask.

"My mom swore me up and down she would never wear one," he says. "Now she's walking around work with that piece of cheese on her head."

The week flies by. Our hotel is in downtown New Orleans, near the French Quarter, and the first few nights we do wind up there, having a drink or two and watching as women on balconies pull their tops off. It's a surreal scene. The streets are mobbed. Music blares from every bar. By night three it's all too much. Paul and I rent a movie on the hotel system and stay in, too exhausted by those 8:00 a.m. press conferences to do anything else. I fall asleep a third of the way into the movie.

The rest of our crew is not so lucky. Many people get put up in a seedy part of town and have to drive close to an hour just to start their day. Photographers are doubling up with each other. Tall Dave and short Jimmy get paired in a room.

"He's so little I'll just slide him in a drawer," Dave jokes, but the truth is—who wants to share a room with a coworker? It's a little too intimate. I'm glad Paul and I are paired together, although we don't actually work much as a unit during the day. He is often with Kevin, another sports anchor, and I am assigned to Dave. It's probably better that way—it gives us something to talk about at night.

As a station, we crank out stories for the specials and find ourselves doing live shot after live shot from another one of those NFL-lifted risers facing the stadium every night. Jane Skinner is there for the FOX affiliate. She's a local reporter, a nice person, I think. Later, when she marries Roger Goodell, who would go on to become the NFL commissioner, I will think back to her standing in jeans and tennis shoes on the riser with the rest of us, just a Milwaukee reporter back then.

The Packers are playing the Patriots and all of the Boston TV stations are there, including the one where I interned. I run into the reporter who was cold to me at that college basketball practice so many years before. Still cold, still unfriendly. Some things never change.

We work so much that week that Kevin starts to get upset. "This is crazy. This is like slave labor," he says. He gets into it with the assistant news director.

"Tough," is about the only response we get. But we are tired. One night on the air I say "Welcome back to Green Bay," when I meant, of course, to say New Orleans. I don't even realize I have said it until we're into the first taped piece and the producer tells me in my ear.

"Sorry, everyone, I misspoke," I say when we're back on live. "Force of habit. Yes, I do realize we're in New Orleans."

We also do many live shots from the team hotel. There is a room, just a generic conference room, they have given to the local stations to use. We try to spruce it up a bit with some green and gold behind us and an artificial plant, but it's just about as boring as can be. Yes, we're live in New Orleans, but with a wall between us and it.

Game day and we're all deciding what to wear. Do we go with casual polos with the station logo or nice dress clothes? Our main anchor Mike Jacobs makes the decision.

"Big event, we have to dress the part," he declares. We put on our nicest duds and head to the Superdome.

We watch from the press box, crammed in like sardines, as the Packers beat the Patriots, 35–21. In the final minutes we are allowed to walk down into the tunnel area and wait to be let on the field.

But as the horn blows and an unreal Packers-win scene is unfolding on the field, the rent-a-cop security guard will not let us through.

"Sorry, wrong pass," he says, pointing to the chart on the wall that shows which pass will get you where.

"But the game is over. We have to get out there," I say. Our photographers are on the field, waiting to meet us and do those on-field interviews you see right after a game—the ones where you get the best stuff because the players are still emotional.

"Sorry."

Despite the protests of the entire group of reporters (at least twenty-five of us) he will not relent, finally giving in only after the best interview time has passed. When we find the photographers, the first thing they say, of course, is, "Where have you been?"

I look for Beebe in the locker room. He's wearing the same hat the store clerk showed him.

"You did it! You got your locker room cap!" I say. He just smiles and nods, unable to speak, his eyes wet. Beebe lost four Super Bowls with the Bills and this is his first victory.

Working inside the Packers team hotel for Super Bowl XXXI. You can see our "set" in the background with one sign and a fake tree. COURTESY OF JIMMY ANGELI

Even though our station isn't the network carrying the game, we do hours of coverage, interviewing players and rehashing every moment of their historic win. Paul gets a shot of Reggie White racing around the field with the trophy in his hands. It's the lasting image I will have of White after his untimely death seven years later from a cardiac arrhythmia.

Paul winds up getting his face on a T-shirt. He's shooting Holmgren being carried on players' shoulders when someone snaps a picture. It turns into a shirt sold around the state, perhaps the country, and there's Paul among a sea of still and video photographers beneath Holmgren, looking up and pointing their cameras at the coach.

We interview happy players on the field for hours. After the game the news director has rented a restaurant right on Bourbon Street for a station meal and we feast like New Orleans kings. There's even a Mardi Gras–type marching band on the street below us to complete the ambience.

The next day I have to hoist myself out of bed for one of those patented 8:00 a.m. press conferences. It's the one where the coach and the MVP wrap things up. Someone asks Holmgren who will design the ring for the champion Packers. He quips that maybe it will be his wife.

Then the Packers are off to a welcome-home celebration the likes of which Green Bay has never seen. I'm in New Orleans, working on the wrap-up piece, so I watch it on the national news from the satellite truck that night. Thousands of people jam the streets as the Packers bus crawls through. It looks to be freezing in Green Bay, snowflakes flying, but it apparently hasn't kept one person at home. "Wow" is all we all keep saying.

Our news director has given us one bonus day off after all of the work, so we have free time to explore. But in fact, Paul and I sleep for half of it, then decide we'd really better try and see something.

The French Quarter is deserted now. It's a cool, rainy afternoon and the whole area seems to have a film over it. There's a tarot card reader on the corner. Oh, what the heck. We go in.

A Packers victory! What a rush. Antonio Freeman is wearing the champions' T-shirt they gave out right after the win. COURTESY OF JIMMY ANGELI

"You two are soul mates, meant for each other," she says. For that she charges us $25. And it wasn't too hard to figure out what to say, I decide, when she saw our wedding rings.

We find a nice, French-style café and get in out of the cold for a cup of coffee.

"Can you believe what we just witnessed?" I ask Paul, sipping a cappuccino.

"I know, that was crazy." He's a Vikings fan and this has to hurt him a little. But he's also conscious of the enormity of the moment for Packers fans.

Super Bowl XXXI is over. Little did we know we'd be doing the same thing again the next year.

THE WHITE HOUSE

APRIL 1997

A FEW MONTHS AFTER THE SUPER BOWL, the Packers are sent to Washington, DC, to do the obligatory smiles and handshakes every winning team gets with the president. I am assigned to go. Now that's a big *wow*, even for someone who feels she's not easily impressed. The White House. I'm not satisfied with anything in my closet, so I go to the mall and buy a pricey suit.

We will be allowed to do live shots from the lawn where the CNN and national reporters usually stand. We can also watch the Packers ceremony, but we can't get any closer than about fifty yards away and we can't interview any players. They are whisked in and out.

Photographer Dave and I have the morning in DC to kill before the team arrives, so we excitedly head to see the major monuments. I haven't been to DC since a fifth-grade safety patrol trip and I'm enjoying strolling along the National Mall, past good old Abe Lincoln and the Vietnam Veterans Memorial, when we realize that time slipped away from us. We race back to the hotel to change, then run to the White House. We have heard security is tight, but I find it shockingly easy to get in. I show my photo ID to one guard at a little stand, not unlike the kind you might find at a state park entrance, and I'm let through. Of course, this is pre–9/11, but it's slightly unnerving how little security there is, at least for the media.

Now we're crossing the big front lawn and being taken through the press conference room where you always see the backdrop of the blue curtain and presidential insignia when the press secretary talks. It's a lot smaller than I imagined, really just one long but not wide room in one of the wings of the building.

We're allowed to set up the cameras in the designated press area while we wait for the team. As we're finishing up I spy a tall man a few hundred yards away under a tree practicing his putting. There seems to be a putting green specifically designed for this purpose under this particular wide oak. I look closer. It's President Clinton. The silver hair is unmistakable. A little surge of excitement flows through me. That's the president of the United States and he's just hanging out relaxing within my view and earshot. It's a cool moment that doesn't last long. He putts a few more minutes, then heads through a side door into the White House, presumably to put on his suit coat and get ready for the team.

Every Packers coach and player is there except for one. Mark Chmura is a staunch Republican and has refused to be near this Democratic president. Jim McMahon is making a statement of a different kind. He was Favre's backup that year but is actually wearing a Bears shirt under his suit jacket, a nod to his 1985 Chicago team that couldn't go to the White House due to the *Challenger* disaster.

We watch the ceremony from our roped-off press area. It's in the Rose Garden and everything seems smaller than it does on TV. President Clinton makes a few remarks, gets a few laughs, and, of course, is handed some Packers gear by Holmgren. And that's it. It lasts all of fifteen minutes. The players go back inside to a private reception. Dave and I and the rest of the press corps are ushered back through the press conference room to the front lawn to do live shots. It's a beautiful spring day in DC. I have requested a live interview with Donna Shalala, the secretary of the US Department of Health and Human Services who used to be chancellor at UW–Madison. She still has a soft spot for Wisconsin and has attended the ceremony in a green and yellow ensemble.

When she strides across the lawn to us, I'm thinking, "Health and Human Services. Health and Human Services." As previously stated,

I'm not much for politics and I don't want to screw this up on the air. I can think of nothing more embarrassing than accidentally calling her the secretary of defense or something. Shalala is a tiny woman with a bundle of dark hair and a big smile.

"We have Donna Shalala, the secretary of Health and Human Services, with us. Donna, thanks so much for your time. I see you're wearing the right colors for the day," I say.

She answers with a warm laugh, talking about how proud she is of the Packers. She admits she still loves Wisconsin and wouldn't have missed the event for anything.

We carry on with the interview and when I say good-bye I breathe a sigh of relief. I did not misspeak her title. I look like I know what I'm talking about.

Brett Favre rarely got dressed up, so wearing a suit was a big thing for him. You can also see Jim McMahon in the back row with his Bears jersey on and President Clinton with a cane due to knee surgery. COURTESY OF JIM BIEVER

The rest of the day is spent recapping the same fifteen-minute photo op again and again. It feels very important to be on the White House lawn. Looking back on the experience, it is not the ceremony that sticks with me. It is the flash of a real human moment—seeing President Clinton playing a little golf—that made me realize how alike we all are, whether we're the most powerful person in the free world or an average Joe. We all need that little bit of private and quiet space under a tree.

SUPER BOWL XXXII
JANUARY 1998

PACKERS GENERAL MANAGER RON WOLF once famously worried about being a "fart in the wind," a one-hit wonder. So it is no surprise to me that I see him at his most joyous when the Packers beat the 49ers in the NFC championship game in the rain to advance to Super Bowl XXXII in San Diego. He walks off the field pumping his arms with two thumbs up and a grin from ear to ear. They are back.

This time our station sends even more people. The game is to be aired on NBC and we expect a win from the heavily favored Packers, which means a long postgame show.

We all fly to San Diego.

Once again we are on the Super Bowl train: an endless series of interviews and press conferences. This time we have contracted with a few other players, including a charismatic defensive back named Eugene Robinson. I will be meeting up with them to conduct one-on-one, away-from-the-field interviews.

Robinson is no problem. He happily goes along with whatever we suggest, including going to a place where people hang glide to watch them run and jump off the side of a cliff, their bodies dipping below the sight line for a minute before the glider's wings catch air and bring them up again.

"Man, they look like bats. Batmen," Robinson says. We get some great video of him watching the hang gliders and commenting on them, with the Pacific Ocean glistening in the background. I always liked Eugene Robinson. That season he had been the best sound bite in the locker room—always smiling, a booming voice.

Several years later, after he leaves the Packers for the Atlanta Falcons, Robinson returns to the Super Bowl. He is caught soliciting a prostitute the night before the game while his wife is back in their hotel room. Is this the same Eugene Robinson I had known? The guy who sailed happily through life? It just proves to me that you can never really know anyone.

One of the other players turns out to be more difficult on the Super Bowl XXXII trip. He seems disinterested in the interviews. One day I am supposed to meet him in the lobby of the hotel. He doesn't show. I call his room. He answers but says he is running late; he'll be there in a bit. I wait. After another half hour I call again. We have places to be, too. Could he come down and do the interview? It will take only ten minutes, and he had agreed to a deal with the station. After making us wait close to another half hour he finally comes down. He had tried to duck us all week. I don't know why some players say they are on board to do these special interviews and then change their minds. Maybe the reality of the pull on their time hits them. Maybe they're just tired from practices and press conferences, and the lure of a bed and a TV is too much to hold up their end of the bargain. Maybe they regret ever signing up to do it. All I know is it makes our job as reporters much more difficult and makes us feel like the old nag in their lives.

The big thing that stands out from media day this year is something that doesn't seem all that noteworthy at the time. The new tight ends coach named Mike Sherman is standing off to the side by himself. No one is interviewing him.

We approach Sherman. He is polite but quiet. We do a brief and unremarkable interview and he comments on how crazy media day is. I get the sense that he doesn't like crowds or the spotlight. That's why I am surprised two years later when he is named Packers head coach. One year after that he adds general manager to his title when Wolf retires.

I often think back to that moment at media day. Sherman's personality was so cerebral, so opposite the affable Holmgren or Ray Rhodes, the player-friendly coach who had the job for one year after Holmgren, that it was hard to imagine him being comfortable in the spotlight of both jobs. He seemed to be more suited to serving behind the scenes or as an assistant coach. Sherman was a good man who had some success, but he was stripped of the GM job and let go altogether by Ted Thompson not long after that. It didn't help that in his last year the team was 4–12.

Back in San Diego, after media day, we pound the pavement for stories: surfing with Travis Jervey, going to John Michels's high school. Sadly for Michels he is inactive on game day. A first-round draft pick who never panned out. I had done a story with him, his wife, and their baby girl the year before. He even played his guitar for us. I felt for Michels: like Mike Sherman, he was a good, solid person who just wasn't the proper fit for that particular job.

Another day we are walking out of the team hotel and a low-level special teams player is standing off to the side, in the sun by a small palm tree. I smile and say hi, and he stops my photographer Dave and me.

"I just can't stand this," he says. "I hate how all of the media are everywhere hounding me. All these interviews and responsibilities. I can't wait for this Super Bowl to be over."

I honestly think he is kidding at first, but he is not. No one is hounding him, not one person. He is a gunner on the coverage units. He is not exactly a household name. I want to tell him to enjoy it while he can, that he would have the rest of his life to live in anonymity and that he would probably be out of football in a few years anyway (he is), but you don't say that to someone. So we nod sympathetically and continue on our way.

We have a trailer set up in the stadium parking lot and spend most of our time there, sometimes so busy that we joke that we simply forgot to take a bathroom or food break. We need to "own" this Super Bowl because it is on our network.

Again many of our crew are lodging in a less-than-desirable part of town, and one night there is a murder not far from them. They can see the blood and chalk line on the sidewalk, as well as the police tape, when they walk from their cars to the hotel. It is a little unnerving for them, to say the least.

Outside the trailer at Super Bowl XXXII, with my favorite staple food, peanut butter, right near me. I'm also wearing the photographer's vest that would put me near the end zone when John Elway did his famous pinwheel.

We jam all week and are ready for a huge Packers victory party. They would be back-to-back champs! But nothing turns out the way you plan. The Denver Broncos come to play. Broncos running back Terrell Davis, despite a headache that sends him to the locker room in the first half, rushes for 157 yards. John Elway finds life in his old legs and pinwheels for a key first down inside the 5, which leads to a touchdown. I am standing right in the corner of that end zone when it happens. There was not enough room in the press box and I had been given a field-photographer pass. Holmgren also loses track of downs and lets the Broncos score late to try and preserve more time for a tying score. It doesn't work. The last play is incomplete from Favre to Chmura on fourth and 6. Elway is getting carried around on his teammates' shoulders. The Packers have lost.

Now we are stuck with a three-hour postgame show and no Packers willing to talk for any length of time about their defeat. We end up interviewing plenty of Broncos. We talk to so many Denver players our news operations manager says in our earpieces that night, "This is a nice Broncos postgame show."

Super Bowl XXXII is over. It is obvious Favre assumes he will be back numerous times, that losing this one is not that big of a deal. That he might not mind if Elway got one because he'll have so many more in the end. He gives a quote after the game saying how young he is, how many years and chances he still has ahead of him. Of course, as we all know, he never returns—in green and gold, or otherwise.

BRETT FAVRE

THE EARLY PART OF MY CAREER was spent covering one major sports figure.

"Brett Lorenzo Favre."

That's how the Packers longtime PR director, Lee Remmel, always introduced him at press conferences. Remmel himself was a treasure. He worked well into his seventies, offering a deep-throated chuckle and a pleasant word for anyone he encountered. Whenever I asked him how he was doing, for ten straight years he had the same answer, "Relatively sober, at least for now."

Remmel had a great deal of respect for Favre, you could tell. We all did. Favre was like a superhero. He could have run for governor and won, even if no one knew what political party he was in. Women swooned, men wanted to be him, kids plastered their walls with his picture. His later fall from grace would stun me, but now it is early in both of our careers. The Packers are going to play a 1998 preseason game in Tokyo against the Kansas City Chiefs. The NFL is trying broaden its fanbase and make itself more global by playing games over the years in countries such as Japan, Mexico, Canada, and England. I've been given a chance to do a rare one-on-one interview with Favre to preview the trip for our new show *Inside 1265*. (The Packers' address is 1265 Lombardi Avenue, a fact that we constantly try to remind people of during the show so they can figure out the title.) This interview will take place in a drab PR office outside of their Lambeau locker room. I'm nervous for my first one-on-one talk with this football god.

Favre is a tall and imposing figure. He's still wearing his red, no-contact practice jersey.

He shakes my hand.

"Do you know any Japanese?" I ask as the camera starts rolling.

"I know one word: *Konnichiwa*," he says, pronouncing the Japanese greeting with his Southern drawl.

"Do you think you'll be recognized in Tokyo?"

"I don't know," he says with a laugh. "I wouldn't mind if I wasn't."

He's beginning to feel the pluses and minuses of being a star. He's just been in a movie with Cameron Diaz, *There's Something about Mary*. Living in a town with a population of less than 150,000, as he does during the season, I can understand that he can't go anywhere without someone pointing, mouth agape.

We head off to Tokyo, the Packers on their charter, Paul and I on a commercial airliner to Japan by way of Detroit. We're being sent together partly so the station can pay for just one hotel room. But there is one other thing: I'm newly pregnant with our first son, Jake, and feeling very sick to my stomach.

"Hang in there, little baby," I say as I pat my belly. Our first day at the hotel and I'm nauseated and jet-lagged. I'm supposed to go to the lobby to see the Packers arriving, but I just need to shut my eyes. Before I know it, I'm fast asleep. Paul takes the camera and shoots the video we need. I'm groggy when he comes back in.

"Did I miss the arrival?"

"Yup, but it's fine. You needed to sleep," he says.

I have a hard time finding food to eat in Tokyo. I don't do fish or meat and there are not many other options. I'm starting to have a pregnancy craving for a grilled cheese. I have to explain to the room service attendant how to make it and I'm thrilled when it turns out OK, but I will struggle through a week of unusual foods.

The backyard of the hotel is a traditional Japanese garden with koi ponds, flowers, and small bridges, and this is where we walk with players while we're interviewing them to try and give a different, non-football feel to everything. Fullback William Henderson is one of our interviewees and I ask him where else in the world he would like to visit that he's never been.

"Oh, definitely Africa," he says, leaning against one of those wooden bridges. "I would love to follow my heritage, trace my ancestors."

As we stroll the gardens, it strikes me how multidimensional many of these players are. Yet we see them as just warriors on the field of play.

We follow the Packers all over Tokyo for three days. They practice on a small field next to a flat-fronted, gray apartment building, and it's humorous to see the middle-aged Japanese women in kimonos, with their dark hair pinned up, peeking out the windows at these strange, large Americans taking up so much space on the tiny plot of grass in front of them.

I have another chance to chat casually with Favre, off camera, just off to the side, before practice begins.

"So what was Cameron Diaz like?" I ask.

"Cool, real cool. The whole experience was great," he says. Then the whistle blows and he jogs off.

We are shuttled around Tokyo on the ultramodern and air-conditioned media bus, but it herks and jerks its way through the crowded streets, brakes squeaking to avoid the next motor scooter or bicyclist. I sit by the window with my eyes closed, feeling sick and willing the tiny baby to forget the fact that we're in a different country and to grow healthy and happy. Paul is next to me and looks at me worriedly.

"Are you doing OK?" he asks with husbandly concern.

"Yeah, I'm just a little nauseous."

When we're not on team duty, we shoot stories on our own around Tokyo, highlighting a Japanese McDonald's with all of its exotic offerings shown on bright pictures in the window (no Big Macs here; instead, they have rice and fish concoctions), the neon lights of the central city, and the overcrowded subway system. We shoot standups in the back of one of the taxis, which are the cleanest cabs I've ever been in, each one with a lace doily over the passenger seats. Paul is loving the tiny neighborhood restaurants that serve sushi day and night, but I opt to stay in and get some extra sleep anytime I can in the slim hotel bed built for just one person.

We have to edit at the CNN Tokyo bureau, which is located on a small street teeming with people commuting to and from other places. There is a constant flow of humanity walking outside the window. CNN is stuffed into a small, colorless space that has a rent-an-office feel to it. Piles of papers are stacked in every corner and filing cabinets overflow with tapes and editing machines. It's a bit claustrophobic, but luckily there is hardly ever anyone there. It seems to be staffed by one or two people on a daily basis—hardly the bustling foreign bureau I had imagined. They kindly guide us to the feed room, and we beam our stuff back to the United States in the middle of the night, US time, meaning our overnight managing editor has to take it in and organize it for the next day's shows.

Game day at Tokyo Dome. A mix of expat Americans and local Japanese are waving flags and blowing horns. The Packers are ahead, but my biggest concern is that there's nothing to drink except Coke. I'm trying not to have any caffeine, not to put anything in my body for the next seven-and-a-half months that will rev up the baby, even for a moment. I'm a little neurotic about it. Then I can't even find water. It's Coke or nothing. Reluctantly, I get a glass of it. This is my memory of Tokyo, I think: being forced to drink a Coke. I'm sitting next to general manager Ron Wolf in the makeshift press box they've stuck in the seats. He smiles at me, tipping his cup of soda my way, and I return the pleasantry, thinking to myself: not fair, men can drink all the Coke they want.

The Packers win the game in overtime, 27–24. This being only preseason, Favre threw just five passes. I don't think he was able to go unrecognized in this foreign land: there were autograph seekers in the hotel lobby morning and night.

Over the years I will have many memories of Favre. People ask me later if I knew he was fooling around even back then. No. There are rumors of Favre and other players hitting the bars in Milwaukee, but I never see evidence of wrongdoing.

In fact, my favorite memory of Favre is him sitting in a middle school gym watching his wife, Deanna, play basketball in a ladies-only league just a few days before he and the Packers take on the 49ers in the 1995 play-offs. He is crouched on the floor of this average school court, next to his agent, Bus Cook. His oldest daughter is running around the gym, entertaining herself doing cartwheels on the sidelines. Favre looks like a husband and father. He watches the game intently. We were doing a story on Packers' wives competing in their own sports, and I interviewed Deanna afterward.

I found her to be stunningly beautiful with her long dark hair and her Mississippi twang. She was very accommodating and told us about how she had played basketball in high school and college. I asked Favre if he wanted to say anything on camera, but he declined. This was one story he didn't want to be a part of; he was happy to yield the spotlight to his wife.

It was a touching moment when Favre shaved his head in support of Deanna as she went through breast cancer treatments in 2004. We had been

Was I surprised to see so many Packers fans in Tokyo? A little. But then again, Packer backers never fail to impress me with their passion and devotion. TODAY'S TMJ4, MILWAUKEE

told Favre wasn't at practice for "personal reasons." All of the reporters speculated on what that could be. Needed a day off to sleep? Or was it something more serious? Then we were informed that Deanna had just gotten results from a mammogram and Favre had gone home to be with her. It was a shocking diagnosis and we would watch Deanna lose her hair over the next year, first wearing a wig and then going with a short, stylish cut.

Coworkers later said Favre's infidelity was well known by everyone in Green Bay. I must have been in the dark even though Favre did do a little light flirting my way, asking me what my middle name was once.

"Victoria. And I already know yours, thanks to Lee Remmel," I shot back.

Twice he threw me passes, and I mean this literally. I was walking across the practice field in the Don Hutson Center as the team was warming up and Favre called out, "Jessie, catch!" The first one I actually held on to, stunning myself.

"Whoa, nice catch," said a male *Journal Sentinel* reporter next to me. "How come he never throws any passes to me?"

The second time Favre did it, I was pregnant and did not want the ball to hit my big belly. I tried to deflect it and, in my clumsiness, had the ball graze my stomach anyway. I worried for a few days that the baby was OK. Like everyone said, Favre did throw a rocket ball.

A few times he gave me a smile from across the field. Once I was holding a stack of papers and they slipped from my hands. Not because I was so floored by him, just because they slipped. When I looked up, he was smirking.

"It wasn't you," I wanted to shout.

Favre's second daughter, Breleigh, was born within a few months of Jake. One day when our kids were just under three I saw Favre in the hallway.

"So how's the potty training going?" he asked.

"Actually not too bad. How about you?"

"Terrible. We can't get her to figure it out."

He was a normal person, a normal dad in that moment, and I could almost forget his superstar status. Whenever people would ask me what Brett Favre was like, I would always tell them about this potty training conversation.

Over the years I watched Favre overcome an addiction to painkillers, win three MVPs, and take the Packers to two Super Bowls. He used to give rambling press conferences with long-winded answers to every question. But he was smarter than most people thought. This was no country bumpkin. That's why watching him spiral downhill was so painful to see.

I always thought he could author a book titled *How to Fall from Grace in Three Easy Steps*. Step one: hold your employer and millions of fans in suspense year after year with your indecision. Step two: go play for your archrival. Step three: take pictures of yourself in the nude and text them to a female reporter.

"Do *you* have any pictures of Favre? You could be on TMZ by tonight!" a friend e-mails me.

"Does his big toe count?" I joke back.

I am so grateful this scandal didn't break while he was in Green Bay and so thankful the most I can say about a personal connection to Favre is that he knows my middle name.

Late in Favre's career I am the sideline reporter for Packers preseason games. I requested a few minutes with him to prepare some sideline material. The PR guy calls me in the morning.

"Brett will be available at 11:00 a.m. Can you get up here that quickly?" Uh-oh, is my first thought. I have two problems. One: we were planning to go on a quick weekend getaway to Door County with the kids and some friends. And two: my parents' car is acting up and that's the one I will have to take if I drive separately. But I can't say no after requesting this.

"Can he make it noon? I'll get on the road as soon as I can," I say.

"Well, he'll be at lunch, but we'll see if we can pull him aside for a few minutes. Call me as soon as you get here."

My husband runs the car over to the gas station to fill the tires and add a little oil to the tiny white car that we joke is about one step up from a go-kart. I jump in the shower and throw on the first clothes I see that don't have to be ironed. Paul and the kids are planning to go minigolfing as soon as they get to our Door County destination, which is about an hour and a half northeast of Green Bay.

"I wish I could minigolf, too, but I want to do a good job at this sideline thing and I need to talk to Favre," I tell the family.

"We understand," says my ever-understanding Paul. "Just meet us there when you can."

I race to Lambeau, calling the PR guy from the parking lot and running inside.

Favre comes strolling to our appointed spot, in sweats, with a toothpick in his mouth. I guess he did just finish lunch. My own stomach is growling, but I need to forget about food right now. We're leaning against the equipment counter in the locker room where they put their helmets and pads to get fixed by a whole staff of equipment specialists.

I know I have only ten minutes with him and a huge list of questions. I'm trying to solicit some info that other people don't already know from his press conferences. I ask him for specifics of his offseason, then turn to a more personal matter. Deanna's stepfather has just passed away, another tragedy in the Favre family, and I want to know if Packers fans responded in any way. He tells me about some of the thousands of cards they got and what some of them said.

This is 2007, Mike McCarthy's second year, and he's brought his own terminology. I ask Favre to explain the differences from Mike Sherman.

He thinks about it for a few seconds before answering in his Southern drawl, explaining that words that meant one thing with Sherman might have a completely different definition under the current regime. I can see that it's not easy to switch coaches.

I thank Favre as my time is more than up. The PR guy was starting to pace.

I head up to Door County and find the family at the beach.

"Mommy!" yells Charlie, running at me with his arms wide open. "Come see my sand castle."

We are sharing a house with some friends and their kids. They're all sitting in the sand together.

"You just interviewed Brett Favre," says our friend. "I mean, you just interviewed *Brett Favre*. That is so amazing."

"Yeah, it's pretty cool, but if you're around him enough you realize he's a regular guy," I reply.

The next day we walk the kids over to the quaint Baileys Harbor library to play "Club Penguin" on the computers and look at some books. I bring all of my Favre notes with me and try to find a quiet spot to organize my thoughts and write some of the thirty-second sideline reports I will be doing. But it's almost comical as Jake and his friend Bennett keep interrupting to ask about this or that, why the computer won't work, or what movie they can check out that night. Big-shot reporter, I'm thinking. Just interviewed Brett Favre and can't get two seconds away from the kids to do it justice. I sigh and pack up my notes.

The Packers were 8–8 the year before. Favre still mostly has the love of the people at this point, but there is a subtle undercurrent of unrest among Packers fans.

That all changes starting with that very season, when the Packers go 13–3 and make it to the postseason. Then the top-seeded Cowboys are upset by the New York Giants and the NFC championship game is coming back to Lambeau unexpectedly. We are in the sports office watching the Cowboys lose and jumping around and cheering like mad. "The NFC championship! The NFC championship!" We are all acting like eight-year-olds. This is sure to mean another Super Bowl run.

The week leading up to the game is filled with anticipation. The Packers host a pep rally at Lambeau and I am asked to be one of the emcees. The stands are mobbed with fans despite a gripping chill. I get there later than I want to only because I have a babysitting issue and need to ask a friend to help out. So I zip downtown to drop the kids at her condo, stopping along the way to pick up a gift certificate at Culver's for my friend (I truly don't know what I would have done with the kids otherwise). Then I race to Green Bay and try to organize my thoughts and notes before taking the stage. I am feeling disheveled. I have on long underwear and a coat that is too much of a drab brown but also the warmest I own. My shirt has a stain on it from some kind of kid-related disaster. My thoughts are scattered and there isn't enough time to really get set. Wing it, girl, I tell myself.

Large heaters are set up to keep us warm, but I am still bundled to the max. We have current and former players join us on stage and also Mark Murphy, who is in his first year as president and CEO of the Packers. Fans go crazy as players talk about the unexpected NFC championship game and a chance to go to the Super Bowl. The show goes OK despite my lack of prep time, and I breathe deeply in relief. Another smoke-and-mirrors TV moment: smile a lot and don't show the world the rough day you've had up until that point.

Then comes the infamous game.

It's the coldest night I can ever remember: a wind chill of minus 23. I'm actually moderately surprised the NFL didn't even consider rescheduling. It's wicked outside—the kind of cold that has you in its grip within three seconds. Favre looks old and cold with hand-warmers stuffed around his face. I have to watch most of the game from the photographers' area because of the huge media contingent. Then right before the end, I move to the Lambeau Field Atrium, which is an open-concept space with a few restaurants and an entrance to the Hall of Fame. The floor is even painted to look like a football field. Hundreds, if not thousands, of Packers fans are in here watching the game on big-screen TVs, looking for some warmth. The Packers have not played well at all. It looks like the Giants will win, but then Lawrence Tynes misses a field goal. And another. People are screaming in disbelief and joy. The score remains tied. Could they really pull this off even though New York has clearly been the better team?

Then Favre throws that fateful interception. On just the second play of overtime, he tries to connect with Donald Driver, but the ball instead lands in the arms of Corey Webster and is returned to the Packers 34-yard line. There will not be a third missed kick. It's over. The Packers lose. The first thing I hear as I walk quickly through the concourse is a man in a blaze-orange hunting jacket saying "F-ing Favre," as he throws his program into the garbage in disgust. The honeymoon is over. We do interviews in a dejected locker room and have a long postgame show, then drive home in stunned silence listening as fans blast Favre, the coaches, and the entire organization on the radio. They blew it. They had home field and they blew it.

When Favre is traded to the Jets that summer, the picture of him in the paper says it all. His eyes register shock as he holds up his New York jersey. He looks like a deer in the headlights. From our standpoint at the station he's now in the AFC and fades into the background a little. In the beginning, we show highlights of every Jets game, but it slows down by midseason. We're focusing on the new young QB, Aaron Rodgers, and the Packers struggle to get to a 6–10 record that year. Some are screaming for McCarthy's and Thompson's heads. Websites are still going in support of Favre. But that won't last long.

A year later Favre goes to the Vikings. The debate in the state invades just about every dinner table and water cooler. Are you in Favre's corner or the Packers'? I'm in the Packers'. I saw how well he was treated in his Green Bay time. He let spite take over and was intent on sticking it to the Packers for no good reason. He had many great years and should have walked away on top, as hard as that is to do. When Favre returned to Lambeau for the first time, the boos were incredible.

Favre talks with Ragnar, the Vikings mascot. Paul is in the background, shooting. If you had told me Favre would wind up in purple one day I would have laughed.

"Forget Shakespeare. To boo or not to boo, *that* is the question," I say on the air the night before the game. Hardly anyone seems to choose the no-boo option. Favre smirks as he tosses his warm-up throws, but there is hurt on his face, too.

By this time I'm doing some side writing for *The Hispanic Journal*, a Milwaukee newspaper. It doesn't pay much, but it gives me a chance to try writing in a whole different way and scratches a newspaper itch.

"Even if Favre and the Vikings sweep the Packers this year, the Packers are in better shape in the long run," I write. "Favre won't have too many years left."

It's not exactly a startling or unusual observation, but it is dead on. Packers fans rejoice when Favre throws an interception in the NFC championship game against the Saints. Paul, the Vikings fan, is both disgusted and heartbroken.

"Well, at least we're used to losing. They're the Vikings," Paul says, trying to console himself.

"Why do you even ponder passing? You could take a knee and try a 56-yard field goal. This is not Detroit, man, this is the Super Bowl," the Vikings announcer says. It will be replayed on Milwaukee radio over and over again as the sports talk-show hosts laugh and Packers fans feel vindicated in their hatred of Favre.

As Favre's final season in Minnesota winds down the following year, I feel sorry for him. His ego has kept him going a few too many years. His final home game for the Vikings takes place in a college stadium after the Metrodome roof collapses under the weight of snow. It seems almost too fitting. He disappears into Mississippi, the sex scandal soon to follow. Favre jerseys are drastically reduced at every Wisconsin store.

An era has come to an end, but sadly. It could have been so much different, is all I keep thinking to myself.

Not long after Favre leaves the Packers I am given a one-on-one interview with Ted Thompson. Someone had told me Thompson had a picture of Favre in his office and I want to ask him about it. Actually, I want to ask him a lot more, including the story of how he was rumored to have gone for a long drive by himself right after trading Favre to the Jets, but I am told by PR I can only ask the one thing about the picture in his office and that's it. This is about the time that people are having trouble even saying Favre's name around Lambeau Field. It feels like he's Voldemort from *Harry Potter*—"He-Who-Must-Not-Be-Named." I myself find I'm practically choking over the name as I ask Thompson.

"So I understand you have a picture of ... of Brett ... in your office? Can you tell us about that?"

He answers that Favre was very special to the organization and that he's proud to have this picture. That's the end of that. I know I can't ask a follow-up.

Over the next few years I try to interview Favre several times, sending out requests to Bus Cook, telling him we just want to give Favre a chance to talk to Packers fans now that water is under the bridge.

He never returns a single e-mail or call.

MIKE HOLMGREN

ANOTHER PROMINENT Wisconsin sports figure, and someone I will get to know and like, is Mike Holmgren. The first words I remember Holmgren saying directly to me are: "Wrong colors for a Green Bay reporter."

It's training camp, and it's hot. I look down to see what I'm wearing: a purple polo with the station's logo and gold shorts. Purple and gold. Vikings colors.

"Unintentional," I say, and he smiles, the lines around his eyes crinkling. He always has a papa bear look to him with his sandy hair and mustache—almost a modern-day Teddy Roosevelt, who himself had the teddy bear named after him. In fact, sometimes I think Holmgren is the father I wish I had, although in reality I know that NFL dads are gone 90 percent of the time. It's just his warm aura that is fatherly and appealing.

I will go on to host *The Mike Holmgren Show* during his final year in Green Bay, becoming one of the first women in the country to host a coach's show alone.

This starts when I have to fill in for the regular host, Kevin Hunt, who has been sent to cover the 1996 Olympics. I do two shows in his absence.

"We have a little extra time to fill. Let me step over here and do my Oprah impersonation and see if anyone in the audience has any extra questions," I say when we find ourselves unexpectedly light during the taping.

"I liked your Oprah comment," Holmgren tells me later. Plans are made (or so I think) for me to host the following year, but when the time is drawing near Holmgren decides he doesn't want a coach's show that season, that it's too much work as they try to repeat as champs. It's his prerogative. I'm in Arkansas visiting my dad and aunts when I get a call with the news: no show. The Arkansas clan has all gone to an Indian powwow on the University of Arkansas campus. Paul and I leave the drumming and walk out into the warm spring air while I process the call. Why is he taking a year off? Did he not want to do it with me? Was this all my fault?

As it turns out, he just needed a hiatus and returns to the show the following season. I'm at a preseason game and he crosses the field to shake my hand. The Packers are coming off a Super Bowl win and a loss. This is the period when Favre is expecting to be vying for a Super Bowl victory many more times. Reggie White is the backbone of the defense. They have a strong running back with Dorsey Levens and a good receiving corps, including Antonio Freeman and Robert Brooks.

"I hear we're doing a show together," he says.

"Yes, I'm looking forward to it," I say—although I'm still a little nervous he might change his mind.

"I'm looking forward to it, too. See you soon."

We tape the show in front of a live audience at an old television station in Green Bay at 9:00 a.m. every Monday after a game. This means leaving Milwaukee at 6:30 a.m. I usually bring a pillow and sleep in the back of one of our producers' cars, especially after I find out I'm pregnant and I'm tired all of the time. I will keep a stack of saltines in the car for my queasiness.

Holmgren and I meet in a small, windowless office before each show to go over a few details. This is the office the general manager usually holds, but he gives it up for us for these ten-minute meetings every week.

"Just so you don't think I'm getting fat," I tell Holmgren early on, "I want you to know I'm pregnant, due in March."

From that point forward he makes a point of asking how I'm feeling each week.

The Packers are coming off two Super Bowl appearances, a win and a loss. This is the year they will lose to the 49ers in the playoffs on a late, Terrell Owens touchdown and Holmgren will leave for the Seahawks. Still, it's a good year. They win eleven games and Holmgren and I dissect each one. We have a system where I set up each play of the highlights and he describes it.

"So it's third and 10 from the 20," I will say.

"Yes. And Favre audibled out of the play *I* had in mind," he says. "As you can see it didn't work so well. His coach was not very happy with him."

The audience laughs. Holmgren is a natural with them and with the players. He's a born leader and communicator.

I never feel he treats me any differently than any male reporter, certainly never feel disrespected as a woman. He has four daughters. He's as cordial and polite as can be. I enjoy my one season with him. We have a player guest on each week. The time Reggie White comes on, the crowd is huge and goes crazy when he walks onto the set. Same for LeRoy Butler.

We have one especially interesting show when Holmgren is caught by a local station flipping off the crowd as he walks to the Packers tunnel. He was mad because someone yelled something derogatory at him after a bad first half of football. I have to ask him about it on the show.

"I let my emotions get the best of me. It shouldn't have happened," he says. People forgive him. There is plenty of applause at the end of the segment.

Near the end of the season we convince Holmgren to bring a member of his family on the show, to introduce them. He brings his dog and

Next pages: The day that Holmgren said, "I hear we're doing a show together." I held my breath until the first taping, scared he might change his mind.

holds her in his arms for two segments. He keeps her treats in a Ziploc bag on the desk in front of us. It's pretty comical.

The one thing I can tell about Holmgren is he's not long for Green Bay. He's too California, and Green Bay is too small for him. It does not surprise me one bit when he leaves. The common thinking is that he would have stayed if he could have been general manager as well as coach, if Ron Wolf didn't already have the GM job locked down. But I always felt nothing would have kept Holmgren in Green Bay. He won a Super Bowl, had a street named after him, and was ready to move on. The general manager part made for a good excuse, in my opinion.

We tape the last *Mike Holmgren Show* of the season. Rumors are swirling that he might leave but nothing has been announced yet. What do we do if he leaves before the show airs? It will look foolish to have us talking about next season. We hem and haw and finally decide I have to tape an alternate ending just in case. I stand in front of the green

It's always great when coaches will show their personal side, even just a little bit. TODAY'S TMJ4, MILWAUKEE

chroma-key wall and say, "Mike Holmgren took a job with Seattle shortly after this taping. Here's some of his press conference in his new city," and we fill the show with that. At least it's fresh material.

I'm actually relieved now that the season is over. I can focus on having a baby. I take a deep breath as we drive back to Milwaukee one last time. Babies "R" Us, here I come. I need to decorate a room, buy a crib, paint some clouds on the ceiling.

But there is still a story I plan to report on. One of Holmgren's daughters,

Calla, is doing a residency at a Milwaukee hospital. Holmgren is very proud that she's going to be a doctor.

"A doctor in the family, how about that?" he has said to me many times.

We arrange the story with Calla. I meet her first thing in the morning and follow her on her rounds at Froedtert Hospital. People don't realize she's famous unless they happen to notice her name tag and ask her about her last name.

"It's 8:00 a.m. and Calla Holmgren has already been up for two hours. She slept at the hospital the night before . . ." is how the piece starts. Calla bounces around from patient to patient, her blond hair bobbing as she happily checks charts and asks patients how they're doing.

"Why do you have a camera crew with you?" one older African American man asks from his hospital bed.

"Oh, well, I'm actually Mike Holmgren's daughter," she says shyly.

His eyes open wide and he sits up a bit.

"Really? Well, that's kind of different, isn't it?" His smile grows wider as she takes his blood pressure and he asks her about her dad leaving for Seattle.

Calla will depart Wisconsin shortly after Mike does. She's now Dr. Holmgren, an ob-gyn.

I will see Mike Holmgren several more times through the years. Right after he leaves for Seattle I'm sent to ask him about his new job. I have now had the baby, Jake, and my maternity leave is up. We fly into the Pacific Northwest where, in stereotypical fashion, it's raining. Pouring, in fact. The Seahawks office is nestled among some tall pine trees. I had e-mailed Holmgren's secretary months before, requesting this interview. Now he comes into the conference room wearing a Seahawks team logo polo. It looks so out of place after all of those years in green and gold. But he's warm as usual and gives me a nice handshake and a smile.

"You had the baby?" he asks.

"Yes, a boy. His name is Jake."

"Congratulations. I really mean that. There's nothing like kids."

We get down to business. I have been given only fifteen minutes for this interview. Flew all the way to Seattle for fifteen minutes.

"So, what do you think it will be like the first time you return to Green Bay?" I ask.

"I don't know if I can even find the visitors' locker room," he says with a laugh.

He returns to Green Bay and somehow finds the locker room. He will actually come back several times over the years. Once it's a game we all think might be Brett Favre's last home game (little did we know he was actually years from retiring). I run to the visitors' locker room after gathering material in the home locker room. Holmgren is just about to get on the bus.

"Mike," I yell. "Got a minute for one more question?"

"Hey, Jessie, how are you?" he says and turns around, his foot still on the first step of the bus.

The main thing I remember from the interview, the part we used on the air was, "If this was his last game, I'm really glad I was here."

I will also see Holmgren in Cleveland after he becomes the Browns president. He's sitting on a golf cart with his agent, Bob LaMonte. LaMonte has never worn socks once in the years I've known him. He's the definition of California cool. I smile when I look down at his feet and see that that tradition has not changed: expensive leather sandals, no socks.

"Good to see you," we all say. LaMonte gives me a hug that picks me up off my feet. Holmgren looks older. I'm sure I do, too.

"How's Kathy? Tell her I say hi," I say. I have always liked his wife, who went through breast cancer shortly after leaving Green Bay.

"You bet I will. What are you up to now? Still covering the Packers, I see?" he says.

"Yes, remember the good old days of *The Mike Holmgren Show*? I'm actually doing *The Mike McCarthy Show* now."

We each go on our way. I always have a warm spot in my heart for Mike Holmgren, who allowed a twenty-eight-year-old woman to ask him questions on his show and never once made her feel like anything less than a professional.

SIDELINE REPORTING

IN ADDITION TO REGULAR WTMJ DUTIES, I held the job as sideline reporter for the Packers preseason games for nine seasons, and I can safely describe it in one four-letter word.

No, not that one.

The word is *work*. It is a crazy amount of prep work for what is, perhaps, five, thirty-second hits. But it was also an incredible honor, a lot of fun, and an intense balancing act as I juggled being a mother and a reporter.

The first summer I was asked to sideline report was also the summer Charlie was born. He was two months old at the first preseason game. Being on the sidelines was something I had never done before and, from a professional standpoint, a great opportunity. From a personal standpoint, it sucked. I reluctantly flew to Atlanta while my mom and husband stayed home to take care of Jake and little Charlie. It would be two nights.

As soon as I landed I had to catch a cab to the hotel where we were having a production meeting. This was pretty important. It was my first time meeting with the New York–based crew I would work with. The Packers had hired a director, producer, and technical people from CBS

Sports to make the broadcasts look more polished. They brought in announcers. Kevin Harlan was a national name and also happened to be the son of the former Packers president and CEO Bob Harlan. Bill Maas was a former Packers player. Then they asked me to be the sideline reporter. I was humbled and I felt I had to at least try it. So off I went. Now I was in the back of the cab and I had to pump. If you have ever been or have ever known a breastfeeding mother you are keenly aware of what I'm talking about. The meeting would take place as soon as I got to the hotel. No time to pump there. I discreetly pull out the battery-operated pump and set up what I think is a well-executed screen: a couple of folders opened wide so the cabbie couldn't see. Plus there is a Plexiglas wall between us and he's playing music. Privacy. I think I'm set. I slip the pump under my shirt and start the process. Suddenly the music turns off.

"What's that noise?" he asks. He is in his twenties. "Is that something I should be concerned about?"

"No, no, no . . . it's . . . it's kind of a medical thing."

"Are you sure?" he asks suspiciously.

"Yes, I'm sure. No worries." But he continues to give me sideways glances the whole time.

At the Atlanta hotel I find out the meeting is pushed back an hour. No need for me to have worried the cabbie then. But someone forgot to book a room for me and I spend the hour milling around the lobby, trying to get the situation cleared up. They think they might have to put me up in another hotel. They have a lot of events happening. They're busy.

"Can I sleep in a closet?" I joke. By the mercy of God, we finally get it settled and I go into the meeting.

The crew is in from New York. The producer looks like an older version of the news producer from *Murphy Brown*. The director, one of the only women in the business, is a petite, blond, no-nonsense, no-makeup, jean-jacket-and-Converse type and a whirlwind of energy. I imagine her spending weekends walking the streets of Greenwich Village. The assistant director is a wise-cracking tall guy who can't go a minute without a sarcastic comment. Handshakes all around in one of the hotel's many generic conference rooms and we get down to business.

Not only will I be sideline reporting, but we have a half-hour pregame show before each telecast. The director's first instruction to me: "If you need a camera on you tell me exactly where you are. Say 'the Packers 20.' Don't say 'I'm standing near the defensive line coach.' See—I don't know where the defensive line coach is. I hate it when sideline reporters do that."

They tell me I'll meet the A-2 on the field. I don't know what this is, but I don't want to tell them that, so I nod and decide I'll figure it out later. (Eventually I find out it's the second audio person: the man or woman who will be in charge of my microphone and earpiece.) I'm feeling intimidated but also excited to give this a try.

But I still have a breastfeeding problem. The next day I pack the pump and head to the stadium. During the pregame crew meal I pull the producer aside.

"You're a father, right?"

"Yes."

"OK, then I feel I can tell you this. See—I just had a baby and I'm still nursing. There are times I might have to pump, hopefully not during the game. I'll be sure to do it right before but just in case I have to run out for a minute you'll know what's happening."

He smiles. "No problem," he says. "Don't worry and just tell me if you have to leave."

I have nursing pads in my bra. Even though I'm not confident I can make it through the three hours of game time, somehow I do. My first sideline interview is with Donald Driver, who just a few weeks before became a father himself for the first time. I don't tell him about my little situation, but I do ask him how it's going with his baby boy before we go on air. At the end of the interview I tag it out with, "Thanks, Donald. And guys: Donald is a new father and he tells me he's changed a total of eight diapers so far." Kevin and Bill laugh in the booth and Kevin adds, "And I think congratulations are in order for you, too, as we understand you just had your second."

The minute the game is over I tell the producer in my microphone, "I'm going to run now. I'll catch up with you later."

"You got it," he says knowingly. I find the closest bathroom and sit fully clothed on the toilet seat, pumping and dumping again.

Sometimes I had to pack for these sideline trips in such a hurry due to baby and preschooler duty that I would get on the plane and hope I remembered everything. Once I grabbed a shirt that said "La Leche League" and didn't even realize it until I unpacked in the hotel room. Not only did it say "La Leche League" (a club for breastfeeding mothers) but it said it in huge letters and had a tasteful drawing of a mom and baby in the act. I had gotten it at a meeting I went to in the basement of a Quaker church in the Riverwest neighborhood of Milwaukee. I found these meetings to be soothing places where you could relax with a group of women and babies and swap stories and not worry if you had to whip out your breast. But now I was in a ritzy hotel with a load of Packers people. Oh, well. I wanted to work out. I put on the T-shirt, jogging shorts, and tennis shoes and went to the exercise room feeling just a little self-conscious in the elevator. Near the treadmills I saw two people I knew: a member of the Packers front office and a male *Journal Sentinel* reporter. The Packers official was striding away on an elliptical and just gave me a nod, but the reporter glanced at my shirt and did a double take. I smiled and said hello and he did the same. I surmised that he might be a bit surprised by my sporting the business of breastfeeding so loudly. He politely never said anything.

My babies grew and I found my groove as a sideline reporter. I was told by the New York producer to provide him a list of sideline ideas—maybe twenty or so—and he'd pick his favorites from there. OK, I thought. I don't want to report on things Packers fans already know about—and they know an awful lot thanks to the nonstop barrage of radio, TV, and print reporters in the locker room—so how can I get original content? There is only one way to do that in my mind and that's to go "into the trenches," so to speak. I had to find the people who really knew the organization and its inner workings. That would be the head trainer, equipment manager, and strength and conditioning coordinator. So I request twenty minutes with each of them that first season and it is so successful I continue to do it for the next nine years.

"Oh, is it time for the annual Jessie meeting?" trainer Pepper Burruss would joke. But he came armed with sheets of notes on things he thought fans might be interested in learning about.

I would make up a list of questions for each one of them, trying to get as specific as possible to pick their brains.

"OK, what's new in the world of helmets this year?" I would ask Red Batty, the equipment guru. "What about that game when Aaron's helmet got wet and his communication system zapped out? Has that been addressed? Does he still wear the helmet?"

These twenty-minute interviews usually took place in the small seating area just outside the locker room and trainers' area. The Packers have several chairs and tables set up a few feet away from the cases where memorabilia is displayed. There are giant pictures of former players and historic Packers moments. It's a pretty nice place to conduct an interview.

Sometimes, depending on the situation, Red, Pepper, or the strength and conditioning coach (this position changed hands several times over the nine years) would also walk me back to his office to show me something. I would take diligent notes by hand and also have a small voice recorder rolling to make sure I wasn't missing anything and could go back and check that the quotes I'd written down matched what they'd said verbatim. These men provided more information than I could possibly have hoped for. It was a sideline reporter's gold mine. They were eager to talk because they do have a lot going on and not many people seek them out to find out about it. They were all personable and fascinating. Not everything they told me made it on the air—in fact, less than 50 percent did, and I had to weed out what I didn't think would work—but this became the main base for the list of ideas I would give to the producer.

Pepper and his assistant Kurt showed me how they taped up Ahman Green's ankle with a Batman sticker on the side per his request. I asked if I could borrow a used tape job and show it to our audience and they saved one for me. This really impressed the guys at the car rental ticket counter in Jacksonville one year when I went to get my wallet out of my backpack and Green's tape job fell out.

I learned from Pepper that the team was using a new video game–type rehab machine where players could basically play a video game while getting rehab work done on injured knees, calves, and so on. The movements they would make with their legs were designed to benefit their specific injury but also to move a joystick around. After my report during a game, Pepper came up to me on the sideline and said the Milwaukee Bucks had just left him a message, wanting to learn more about the machine.

Pepper taught us all about a new system of taping injuries called "Kinesio taping"—something Olympic volleyball players had used—and we shot a whole piece on it that aired during the halftime show.

He shared that Jordy Nelson's grandma had sent pies to the team a few days before the Super Bowl and we used this on the air, with a few Pepper-provided photos.

I grilled the strength and conditioning coaches on what they did with players both individually and as a group. We learned they had all tried yoga, for instance. But the best stories I got from strength and conditioning coach Mark Lovat came from just looking around his office. One year, I noticed a cleat with a special weight attached to the back. After asking about it, he told me it was Donald Driver's; Driver liked to run with it for an extra workout. The next week we borrowed the shoe and showed it, along with a few comments from Driver.

Another year Lovat had a big tub of uncooked rice sitting next to his door—just plain old rice. What in the world could that be for? Turns out when you put your hand deep into a bucket of rice and turn your fist—just grab and turn, grab and turn—it gives your forearm a great workout. Lovat had seen baseball trainers use it and he brought it to the Packers. Another sideline report, after they allowed us to borrow the rice.

Equipment guru Red Batty gave me so many great ideas over the years. We did pieces on helmets, cleats, jersey styles, and even the differences in footballs. Did you know some quarterbacks like their footballs scuffed more than others? Red told us that Favre had a smiley-face sticker inside the top of his helmet and also shared with viewers what the new, NFL-mandated green stickers on the back of helmets mean (they indicate which helmet has the communication system inside). He told us how some coaches were skirting the rules on field goals: If you had your quarterback as your holder, or had your holder wear the quarterback's helmet, you could call in a fake field goal or extra point at the last second. The NFL was cracking down on this and needed to make sure the holder was not wearing the wrong helmet.

This was not the only way I gathered information, though. I started early in training camp with a folder of sideline ideas. Sometimes a feature story in the newspaper would catch my eye and I'd put my version of that in. I would also scour the media guide as soon as it came out, looking for personal tidbits about players. Perhaps they collected pet turtles or had a degree in something unusual or a brother or cousin who played on another team. I would write all of this down. Then I would think about the opponent for each game. Was there a Packers or Wisconsin connection? When the Packers played the Cleveland Browns, for instance, and former Badger Joe Thomas was newly drafted, I called the Browns PR department and they set me up with a quick phone interview with Thomas that turned into a sideline report.

I appreciated the fact that the producer gave me full control of my reports, but it was also a daunting task each year. I wanted to present twenty (or more) good ideas that could actually make it on. No one was helping me. This was all on me while I was still juggling my regular reporting duties, *The McCarthy Show*, and, oh, yes, being a mom and shuttling kids to various summer activities or taking them swimming for the day. I did plenty of media-guide reading at the pool.

Once I had my big list, I would e-mail it to the producer about two weeks before the game and he would write back with comments about each report: like this one, don't like this one, think this one is too old, love this one but it would be better with a graphic, etc.

We'd narrow it down to the top five or six ideas for each game and I'd set to work fact-checking (sometimes calling Red or Pepper back for clarification or talking with a player if it involved him) and writing out the report on note cards. Everyone does this in his or her own way: some reporters just write key words or ideas; some write what they're going to say word for word. I prefer the latter. I would write the whole sideline report on a four-by-six-inch note card and tuck it into a fanny sack to have close to me. I would rehearse it a few times sitting on my hotel bed the night before the game and tweak the wording if I wasn't happy with it. The goal was to make it sound conversational—and I didn't have to stick to the exact wording on the air if I didn't want to—but having it basically written in my head helped me and I could visualize my index card as I was going along.

Another way I gathered sideline material was just by listening to chatter in the locker room. Once, one of the wide receivers made a passing reference to hanging out with the other wideouts in the offseason on a trip. After the group interview I pulled him aside. Where had they gone? How many receivers? Turns out it was a great story: Jordy Nelson had invited the whole gang down to the farm where he grew up in Kansas to "teach these city boys a thing or two about farm life." The players brought their wives and everyone had a blast down on the farm for a few days. OK, that's great, but a story like that needs some sort of visual. Did anyone take pictures? Oh, yes, Brett Swain's wife was the resident photographer. I asked the PR people to ask Brett for her e-mail address, and Mary Swain came through with the greatest pictures of these well-known Packers with their arms up a cow's behind as they learned how to artificially inseminate Bessie and her friends.

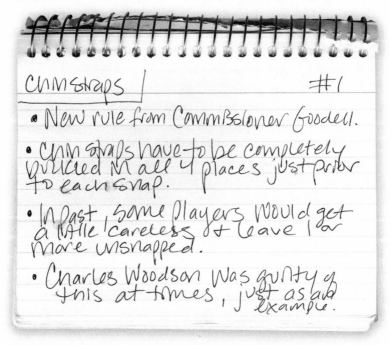

An example of the notes I kept close to me for sideline reporting

One thing I never knew was exactly how many sideline hits I would have per game. And I also didn't know if I would have a "pre-kick" hit. Sometimes they needed me to fill thirty seconds right before kickoff, but sometimes the national anthem and the main announcers used up that time. It all depended on how the commercials were stacked and how that NFL stadium was timing its pregame. So there were several times when the producer would say to me the night before the game, "Oh, and I need a pre-kick hit from you. Can you come up with something good?" This was the ultimate pressure. One night to think of something new and different. We didn't want to use a sideline report that involved a prop or graphic here because there wasn't enough time; we had to be very punctual on the timing to get to the kickoff. In fact, the producer would even talk into my ear, saying, "Twenty seconds . . . ten . . . five, four, three, two, one," to count me exactly to thirty seconds. Now that's a heart-pounding experience—but exhilarating, too, if you can nail it at thirty. (If not, heaven help you.) I liked flailing around for a pre-kick report. One time in Kansas City I had no idea what I would do until we had our morning meeting with Coach McCarthy and he told us how he had gone to visit his daughter—a freshman at Kansas—the night before. Boom! There's my thirty-second report. Coach drives to KU and takes his daughter out to dinner—it humanizes him.

Another time in Cleveland the Packers had just returned from the White House and I was trying to find a sideline report about the visit that was different from anything anyone else had reported. I was talking to one of the Packers employees in the hotel lobby and asked him how meeting the president went. He mentioned that offensive coordinator Joe Philbin had gotten a special handshake and thank-you from President Obama after telling Obama his son was serving overseas. Another humanizing moment, but I needed to confirm it with Philbin and get some more information, so I camped out in the hotel lobby—skipping dinner with the rest of the crew—so I could catch Philbin when he inevitably walked through to go out to eat.

"Joe!" I sprang up from my seat as soon as I saw him. I asked him about it and he gave a delightful account of what happened, including the full exchange between him and the commander-in-chief. It was a very nice report the next day. Having gotten to know Philbin over the seasons, I was heartbroken one year later when another of his sons drowned near Oshkosh. In fact, I saw him just days after the tragedy. I stopped him in the Lambeau Field Atrium. "I'm so sorry. I think I speak for all of Wisconsin when I say we all are," I told him, my voice breaking with grief. "Thank you, thank you," he said, giving me a hug as tears dripped from our eyes.

As for my sideline reports, there were as many misses as hits. Once I was showing viewers a new piece of training equipment that the trainers had been kind enough to drag onto the sideline, and I had no monitor. (It was always a crapshoot whether or not someone would set up a monitor so I could see the broadcast or not.) I kept on blabbering away about this new bike-like device, but I wasn't watching the tally light—the little red light on the camera that lights up when you're on and turns off when your camera is not "hot." When I watched the replay of the game the next day I was really disappointed in myself. The director kept switching back to the action on the field (as she should), but I was unaware that what I was saying about the bike didn't make sense unless you were nearby while I did it. Remember to watch the tally light, I scolded myself.

There were often times when something I had done a lot of legwork for never made it on the air at all. I once called and had a long conversation with Favre's personal trainer in Mississippi. He told me a lot of specifics about different strength exercises he was doing with Favre in one of those offseasons when Favre's age was being questioned by fans. I thought I had a really solid sideline report about it and the producer asked the graphics people to make a full-screen graphic with specifics, such as the exercises he did and for how long—leg squats fifty times, medicine ball thirty minutes, etc.—but it never made it on. It kept being bumped from one game to the next.

"We'll get it on next week for sure," the producer would say. But as the final preseason game wound to a close, we still had not found time for it.

"Sorry, Jess, Favre's trainer is just not going to make it," said the producer in my ear. I was disappointed, but I also understood that the main purpose of a preseason game was not to show what Brett Favre did in the offseason but to show the game on the field.

A lot of the timing for my reports depended on whether the Packers were on offense or defense and if they were close to the red zone. We never wanted to start a sideline report when they were potentially close to scoring because fans rightfully wanted to hear Kevin Harlan's voice describing the action, not me talking about the latest innovation in cleats. We also wanted a story involving an offensive player to be put on while the offense was on the field. Simple, huh? But it's not so much the case when the action is constantly changing.

"OK, we'll come to you if they get a first down," the producer would tell me. Then guess what? They had to punt. No report.

"OK, you're next after this play... unless they go deep." And what do you suppose would happen? Bomb to the end zone.

"You're really next—Kevin and Rich will throw it down to you." (Former Vikings, Redskins, Chiefs, and Raiders quarterback and NFL MVP Rich Gannon had succeeded Maas.) Then someone would get an interception and the tide of the game would change and I'd be on standby again.

When I knew they were coming to me, I would review my note card from my fanny sack and get into place. We would try to get a good background—maybe it was the player we were talking about on the bench behind me or the action on the field. Then I'd take a deep breath and wait. I liked to keep the note card in my hand, just out of camera sight, as a crutch. I always feared having a sudden brain lock and not remembering a thing I was going to say, so just holding the card in my hand made me feel better. When we went to video or a tighter shot of the player or coach I was talking about, I could read directly from the card, too.

It's a real art to do this while looking natural and relaxed and keeping a general eye on the action behind you. I have tremendous respect for the men and women who perform this feat week after week, especially those covering both teams. I had to focus mainly on the Packers, but if you're the *Monday Night Football* sideline reporter you've got to know your stuff on both teams and hustle from one sideline to the other—all while a producer is in your ear.

Once we almost had an embarrassing blooper. The A-2 was hustling around, trying to get the microphone ready, and when he handed it to me the mic flag and the words "Packers Television Network" were upside down. But we were about ten seconds to air.

"The mic flag, the mic flag," I yelled to him.

"Oh, s——," he said and ran over, dismantling the microphone, turning the flag around the right way, and reassembling it in record time.

"Now let's go downstairs to Jessie Garcia," Kevin Harlan said and I started talking as the A-2 guy feigned fainting just off to my side. It was all I could do to stop from laughing.

"Oh, my God," he said when we had finished. "Do you realize how close we came to being all over YouTube with that?"

Thank goodness we weren't.

A word here about Kevin Harlan, who has called professional sports all over television and radio for years. He was the most genuine and professional person I could ever have hoped to work with. When people asked me what he was really like I could only say that he was exactly like his father. Both would ask you questions with real interest and would look you straight in the eye. As a father himself, Kevin was so committed to his children that he often took the last flight to whatever city we were in so he could attend a concert/basketball game/church event with his family. Occasionally this drove the producer crazy, as Kevin could cut it a bit too close, sometimes flying in the morning of a game. He was lucky bad weather never kept him grounded because I wasn't sure what they would have done for a play-by-play announcer had he not made it in, but his tardiness was a direct reflection of his desire to spend time with his family.

I met his wife, Ann, at a restaurant in Kansas City. Usually once a preseason the Packers would offer to take the whole TV crew out to eat. This time we were dining at a nice steak place and Kevin brought Ann along. Blond, well put together, and tan, she was all-American pretty but immediately as genuine as Kevin. That same year the Harlans asked me to interview their daughter during our pregame show. Olivia Harlan was Miss Teen Kansas and they thought it would be fun if I started the interview by not saying her last name and just introducing her as Miss Teen Kansas, then slowly revealing that she was Kevin's daughter and Bob's granddaughter.

Olivia showed up in a smashing red dress. I, on the other hand, was having an off day. I realized when I got to the stadium I had no hairspray or gel. It had rained off and on all day and my hair had been alternately wet and frizzy. I felt like I looked terrible. Then the stadium had provided nothing but heavy meat dishes for reporters to eat. Being a vegetarian I was going on a few dinner rolls for sustenance. I wasn't feeling at the top of my game and almost chuckled when Olivia told me she wanted to be just like me one day.

The interview went well and we did the slow reveal of her name, ending with her putting on a Cheesehead and waving to Wisconsin. I felt good about it until I got home and watched the broadcast. Bad weather had come through Wisconsin at that exact moment and the Olivia Harlan interview consisted of me saying, "And we have Miss Teen Kansas joining us," then two minutes of our weather guy cutting in saying, "We're sorry to interrupt the pregame show, but we have tornado warnings in the area," with graphics of red and green rain all over the screen. When they cut back to me and Olivia, all you saw was her wearing a Cheesehead and waving for about two seconds before it went to commercial. So much for our surprise.

The summer of my final year of sideline reporting, 2011, we were on our annual family vacation to Door County, and Paul and I had gone to see an outdoor play at the American Folklore Theatre, a gorgeous spot in the woods in the middle of Peninsula State Park. Jake and Charlie went to the drive-in theater with my parents. As we walked out of the show, *Lumberjacks in Love*, I saw Kevin, Ann, their son Robert, and Olivia and her boyfriend.

"Jessie! Did you just see this show? Wasn't it wonderful?" Kevin asked.

"Well, hello there. Fancy meeting you here," said Ann. Olivia came over to talk and introduced her boyfriend. I introduced Paul and we all strolled to the parking lot chatting away. When we left Paul said, "Wow, Kevin Harlan is really a good guy."

"I told you so," was my answer.

Rich Gannon was also personable and never acted like a big-shot former MVP. One time in San Francisco he and I had flights back to the Midwest at about the same time and our producer suggested we ride together. I was driving but needed gas. We pulled over near the airport and I was about to jump out and pump, but Rich stopped me.

"What are you doing? I'll do that," he said.

"It's OK, Rich. I can pump gas."

"Oh, no you don't. I got it." As I watched him fill the tank out the side-view mirror I thought to myself, "An NFL MVP is pumping my gas. That's pretty cool."

When we got to the airport, people started recognizing him.

"Are you Rich Gannon? Can I have your autograph?" I smiled at him and waved as he signed, as I headed anonymously to the gift shop for some gum and a magazine. When I got back home I told Paul, the Vikings fan, about Gannon pumping gas for me and he called his brother and told him. Paul wasn't easily wowed by much, but anything involving the Vikings still got to him.

I had a love-hate relationship with the producer, as many producers and on-air talent do, I suppose. He would arrive with his laptop and pages of notes, but it was like pulling teeth to get him to respond to some of my queries. He would write back on the initial story-idea e-mail, but often I would have follow-up questions and I wouldn't get a response until the night before the game . . . or the day of, when I cornered him in the truck.

Part of our rocky relationship was my fault as I made the eager-beaver reporter mistake of talking to him too much in those early years. I had never done sideline work before and was unsure how much I should be reporting back to him during the game. In other words, if I saw something interesting happening around me, should I tell it to him into the microphone (this is not broadcast over the air—just to the truck where the producer and director sit) every single time? At first I told him everything.

"The defensive backs coach was just reaming out the secondary . . . do you want me to do a report on it?"

"I have an injury update for you."

"Would now be a good time to do that one sideline report we talked about?"

After a while I would get an exasperated, "Yes, Jessie?" with a heavy sigh whenever I said his name. I felt like the overeager first-grader who raises her hand to answer every question. I learned to shut up for most of the game, which both helped me and hurt me. It lessened the chances of hearing exasperation in his voice, but I got on the air a lot less. Sometimes almost a whole half would go by without him seeming to remember me at all.

One year the Packers were playing Tennessee at Lambeau and a huge storm came through, sending both teams back to their locker rooms for shelter. We tried to fill time while waiting to see if the game would resume.

"There are hundreds of schoolkids in the Packers tunnel area who were supposed to put on a halftime peewee football exhibition. Do you want me to interview one of them or the coach?"

"No—too boring," he answered.

"It's very visual, though. They're all crowded around trying to fill time right now."

"No, thanks."

In the meantime I can hear Kevin and Rich struggling to fill minute after minute of empty air.

"Jeff Fisher [the Titans coach] has just come onto the field to inspect the footing. Want me to talk to him?"

"Hmm ... let me think about it. . . . No, we'll take a pass."

"Are you sure? He's right here and he's about to walk away."

"Well, OK. Go ahead."

I grabbed Fisher and held him hostage for the next ten minutes, asking questions to kill time. A few years later we were all reminiscing about the game and the producer said, "Remember when we got Fisher? That was great stuff!"

"Yes, but you didn't want it!" I was thinking to myself.

We would always have a production meeting the night before a game. This consisted of the producer, the director, and several other crew members, such as the assistant director and the graphics guy. These meetings were held in a hotel conference room in whatever city we were in. First, the producer of the pregame show would hand out scripts and we'd go over them page by page. Then we'd talk about the game itself and the halftime show. These were very factual, get-down-to-business meetings with not a lot of idle chatter. The crew would go out to dinner afterward and we'd get one good night of sleep before the game, but we could never sleep in too late because we had a meeting with the head coach in the morning.

I only wish all football fans could be a fly on the wall for these meetings. You would never, ever get that much info from a press conference. The coach would come in, shake hands with all of us (this meeting now included Kevin Harlan, if he had flown in yet, and Rich Gannon), and plop down at the head of the table. Then Rich would ask him about twenty questions—things like "So what do you think of so-and-so? How has he looked in camp so far?" or "On paper you're a little thin at this position. Do you feel that way, too?"—and McCarthy would give the most honest, interesting answers, mentioning things he would dance around in any group-interview situation. This was all for background for the announcers. We took notes with paper and pens, but it was not being recorded anywhere and the unspoken rule was that we would use this info as part of a report, not directly quote him. You wouldn't say, "McCarthy told us this morning he's looking old." Instead you might phrase it, "We met with Coach McCarthy this morning and they might have some concerns at that position. At some point they'll have to get some new blood there."

McCarthy would essentially go through his whole roster, giving detailed accounts of each player if Rich asked him to. The producer would throw in a question or two at the end and I was free to ask something, too—but I felt the pressure to keep it short, as the coach was always on a tight timetable and the main hosts and producer were considered the experts.

After this meeting we were more or less free until midafternoon, when a driver would come to pick up the announcers. I would often try to go running midmorning, once bumping into Ted Thompson on the Vanderbilt campus before the Packers played the Tennessee Titans. Then I would retreat to my room and order room service for lunch so I could get in a little more study time. I always tried to shut my eyes and will my body to get into that half-sleep mode for fifteen to twenty minutes before a game, too. This required unplugging the phone in my room and turning off the cell phone or I was sure to be interrupted. I felt like Holly Hunter in the beginning of *Broadcast News*, when she unplugs everything.

In addition to the pre-prepared sideline reports, we would request three or so players to join us on the sideline for live interviews. The producer made this request and never knew for sure if it would be approved until late in the week, so I generally would not find out who I was interviewing until the night before or the day of the game. My job was to think of five or six interesting questions that Packers fans might want to know the answers to.

I would start by just thinking freely about the player, often while pacing around the hotel room. What were the biggest things going on with him right now? Did he have a position change or was he coming off an injury? I would make a list of potential questions on a yellow legal pad and then look at my bible—the "Packers Off-Season Notes and Records Book." God bless the PR staff for compiling a list of achievements the player had already accomplished and milestones he might be near to breaking. I usually wanted the sideline interview to be a mix of looking back and looking forward, and I also wanted to ask the player some questions about his particular position and some about the team as a whole. And me being me, I also wanted to bring a personal side note to the table. I did this with mixed success. Occasionally I was able to unearth something good we could talk about: the fact that Charles Woodson ran the stairs of the stadium alone with headphones on as a workout, for instance. At times I felt the interview was more generic and sometimes I simply ran out of time and the producer would be telling me, "Wrap it up . . . wrap it up now!" in my ear.

I learned over the years not to save your best question for last because it might not make it on. I always think of an interview as a slow warm-up, followed by the key question or two, and then a fill-in—accordion-style, meaning it could be a lot or a little depending on time—the rest of the way. And if you can end with a laugh, so much the better.

Once, while talking to Ryan Grant, we noticed that Clay Matthews kept popping up in the background of the shot—photobombing—and Grant and I joked about that. Grant also had a pencil tucked behind his ear during the interview and the producer said in my earpiece, "Is he doing crosswords? Ask him about the pencil."

At the end of the interview I said, "Before I let you go, Ryan, the guys in the truck want to know what the pencil is for. Are you working on some crossword puzzles on the sideline?"

"No, no," he said with a laugh. "I'm charting plays for the offense, helping the coaches out."

"OK, well, we better let you get back at it," I told him and he tipped his pencil to us in a little salute and ran off.

Once again, it's funny how you remember the bad parts of interviews—or the parts that didn't get on. I once got a lot of praise for an Aaron Rodgers interview I did during a preseason game, but I was silently chastising myself for not asking him about an offseason trip I knew he had taken with a few other teammates to see the Kentucky Derby. I had felt the interview was going too long and decided to wrap it up, but almost immediately, as I was thanking him, I was thinking, "Damn, he might have had some good stuff there. You should have kept on going." I slapped myself around internally for days and couldn't accept any compliments about the rest of the interview.

Another tricky thing on the sideline is balancing your needs with those of the PR department. You have to tell them when you're ready to interview a player and they walk over to him, ask him if he's ready, and bring him to you. Understandably, they then expect you to interview him ASAP, but this doesn't always happen. As I stated earlier, the flow of the game dictates everything, and if the Packers are suddenly in the red zone the producer will not come to me, no matter who I have standing beside me. If there's an interception or sudden turnover and the other team is now on offense, it may change whether or not we start an interview. So there have been numerous times when the PR guy has gotten the player and the player has come to me and I have had to tell him to stand by. As you can imagine this doesn't go over well with the PR staff.

"How much longer? Tell the producer we can't wait much more. I'm not going to make him stand here."

So I will say, "You have to come to me soon. I can't hold him. They're getting anxious."

And the producer will say, "Apologize to Player X from the truck and tell him we'll come to you guys just as soon as we can after this break."

And I will say, "Player X: we're all so sorry for making you wait. Our producer in the truck apologizes and thanks you for your patience. They promise we're next after this commercial."

And Player X, who is usually nice, will say, "Hey, no big deal."

Although sometimes Player X might divert from that script and say instead, "I'm going back over there. Tell [the PR guy] when you're ready." And then I'll feel bad, not to mention that they will inevitably be ready as soon as Player X has walked away.

Part of my job is also to interview the coach at halftime, so by the second quarter I am already thinking about what I want to talk about in my three questions. I want viewers to get some information from him that is relevant to what they have just seen. For instance, when the quarterback has been sacked repeatedly this is obviously a hot topic and I would need to say, "Some protection problems for the offensive line out there. What did you think of the job they did in the first half?"

I once asked the coach something like this and he responded along the lines of, "If we don't get Favre out of there, he's going to get killed." But that kind of honesty was rare. Usually you would get a little less forthcoming answer like, "Yeah, I was disappointed they didn't hold up better, but I won't know more until I look at it on film."

This was often the answer from coaches: they always needed to look at more film before answering. I learned early on not to ask about a specific lineman, for instance, because there was no way the coach was going to have his eye trained on one guy for the first half, so that would be a wasted question. You need to go more big picture with questions: a general theme on the offense, defense, or special teams and one specific thing they did well or poorly in the first half. If you have time, you can then sneak something in about what he was looking for in the second half, or how much Rodgers would play in the third quarter, or something the viewer didn't know yet, and then you would thank him and throw it back up to the guys in the booth.

Most of the time these halftime interviews were conducted live. I would have to watch the Packers tunnel and say, "Here he comes . . . ," when I saw McCarthy striding down the tunnel with his right-hand man. I would have to jump into immediate question-mode. Ninety percent of the time I would ask McCarthy (or the player I was interviewing) whatever I wanted, but there were times the producer's voice would pop up in my ear and tell me what he wanted me to ask. When I was interviewing Jeff Fisher, that day of the rainstorm, the producer said

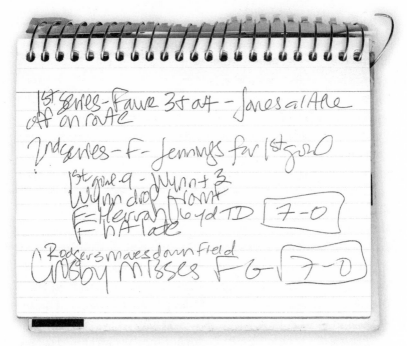

I also had to write down important plays during the game so I could think about what to ask the coach at halftime.

quietly as Fisher was talking, "Fisher played for the Bears. Ask him what he remembers about the Packers rivalry."

And I regurgitated like a monkey, "Jeff, you used to play for the Bears. What memories do you have of playing the Packers and this rivalry?"

It reminded me of another scene from *Broadcast News*, when Hunter feeds the blow-dried anchor the words right before he says them on the air.

Sometimes I might ignore the producer, though, and continue with my planned line of questioning. It would all depend on how I was feeling about the flow of the interview at that time.

We had plenty of funny moments. In Nashville, the stadium crew had planned some kind of snazzy halftime show and the lights went out just as I was about to interview McCarthy.

"Well, Kevin, I'm standing here in the dark with Coach McCarthy as a laser light show is just about to begin," I started. Then halfway through the interview a giant cannon went off near our heads, causing both McCarthy and me to jump—and my eardrum to ring for days.

The night of the Lambeau rainstorm we filled for two hours until they decided to resume the game. At one point Kevin tried to throw down to me, but I couldn't hear him. I was still talking off to the side with one of the crew members.

"Jessie—are you there?" he said. "We thought you were talking to yourself for a minute."

"Kevin, we've been on the air so long—at this point anything is possible," I said with a laugh.

It seemed like I always had a different cameraman, cable runner, and audio person. These were usually men, but at one game the cable runner was a woman and we wound up having a long and very interesting conversation on the sideline about the pain of childbirth.

"If people only knew what we were talking about down here," I said. "They look down from the stands and think we're discussing the intricacies of Mike McCarthy's offense."

Once I completely forgot one of my very detailed note cards at the hotel. It was for a sideline report about Favre and Hurricane Katrina. I didn't have my safety net without the card. I ad-libbed the piece and

Usually I interviewed the coach live, but on this day the camera near the end zone wasn't working, so I took notes as I crossed the field and did the report from a different camera afterward. TODAY'S TMJ4, MILWAUKEE

didn't screw it up too badly, but when I got back to the hotel there was the little rascal, the lone card, sitting on my bed.

"I missed you!" I shouted in the empty hotel room.

Overall, during my nine years of sideline reporting, I found it to be challenging and rewarding but also a lot less glamorous than people realize—but isn't that the case with most things in life?

MIKE McCARTHY

MIKE McCARTHY HAD FIRST been with the Packers in 1999. I barely crossed paths with him then. He was the new quarterbacks coach under Ray Rhodes and lasted just one season. But after stints as an offensive coordinator in New Orleans and San Francisco, McCarthy returned to Green Bay for his first head coaching job. Ted Thompson had just fired Mike Sherman. This was an important hire for the second-year general manager and some considered it a gamble to go with a guy devoid of head coaching experience. But Thompson would always say he and McCarthy clicked right away and he thought McCarthy brought "Pittsburgh macho" to the team. In 2006 Mike McCarthy became the Packers fourteenth head coach.

As I enter the second half of my sportscasting career, I am asked to host the coach's weekly half-hour television program, *The Mike McCarthy Show*, along with former Packers center Larry McCarren, one of the best football analysts and brightest guys I've been around, who also has a pinkie finger horrifically bent from football—a perpetual reminder of his playing days. The three of us get to know each other pretty well through the years.

I can tell I am going to like McCarthy from the first day we have to shoot promos. I am sent to training camp to tape these with him immediately after practice. It is a hot day and he is being given numerous directions by the photographer.

We tell him his line. It is one of his first days on the job.

"I guarantee you access to the Packers you won't get anywhere else. It's your team and your show," he repeats over and over, looking at the camera and pointing, as the cameraman has told him to do. McCarthy is wearing shorts and a Packers polo. Afterward, we stroll to the sideline where some family members are watching.

"Jessie, this is my daughter Alex and this is Alex's mother," McCarthy says. His daughter is sixteen and model-gorgeous. His ex-wife is with her. She's very pretty, too, in a mom way, with long auburn hair and a pleasant smile.

"Hi, how are you?" I ask both of them. Later, while McCarthy is signing autographs I turn back to his daughter. "I know your dad has been a coordinator for years, but can you believe he's the head coach of the Packers now and all of these people want his autograph?"

"I know, it's so weird. He just seems like, you know, Dad," she says.

The next day we have to shoot more promos inside. It's me, Larry, and McCarthy. We're all wearing suits and standing in Curly's Pub, a Packers-themed restaurant at Lambeau with football-shaped light fixtures, cleat-inspired ketchup holders, and black-and-white pictures from yesteryear on the walls. It's here that the show will be taped. McCarthy delivers his line and ends with, "Only on Today's TMJ4 [our station's call letters]." Then he ad-libs, "That's my favorite part," and we all crack up. The promotions people will decide to keep this in, offering a humorous touch to the whole thing.

We have our first show. It's taped in front of a live audience. Larry and I take turns interviewing McCarthy for the first segment, I interview a player for the second, and Larry works with the telestrator, detailing a play with McCarthy, for the third. The fourth segment is for audience questions, which people in the restaurant can ask directly or e-mail in. McCarthy is used to being interviewed, but as a coordinator or assistant he never had to sit in front of a live audience. Plus, he has to wear makeup—just light powder and foundation, but he hates it.

He sweats through that first year with the makeup lady running onto the set between segments to dab his forehead. The makeup artist is a mom who has to bring her daughter in a BabyBjörn one day, patting and wiping McCarthy's face while the smiling baby looks back at us. She also does my makeup those first few years, and she doubles as a hairstylist. One week she offers me a trim in the back room of Curly's Pub, so I bring one of Charlie's big plastic catchall things that goes under a high chair and we do a haircut over that right before the show starts.

In the beginning I have lofty aspirations for the program—probably too lofty. I try to organize local cheerleading groups to come up with a Packers cheer and send in the video to us that we will use going into and coming out of commercial breaks. I also ask some Green Bay cheerleaders to join us live. They are very gracious, especially when I tell them that the show is taped at 7:30 a.m., and there they are, pom-poms in hand, outside of Lambeau Field as the first bits of sun creep over the nearby houses. But the cheerleader experiment doesn't last long. It takes a lot of effort to coordinate these groups. Some say they will send something and never do, and I'm constantly reminded by our crew that this is a coach's show and the coach himself has very little time. I understand and appreciate how busy he is. This is training camp and his day is packed to the second, so I give up championing the cheerleaders and we focus on trying to keep things tight and moving along so Coach won't have to be there long. The audience is seated and ready to go when he gets there and all we have to do is walk out and start the tapes rolling.

Over the years the show evolves. We change sets and move to a more open-air spot two floors up. We switch the guest segment so Larry will ask most of the questions and I will be in the audience to facilitate a fan question or two. The reason for this is never fully explained, but I get the sense that some people at Larry's station in Green Bay feel I'm not asking "football enough" questions because I like to inquire about the players' kids, background, or hobbies in addition to basic football. My belief is that there is an audience for this, people who want to learn something new about the player or coach aside from just the Xs and Os. I feel a little insulted about getting bumped from the main part of the player interview, but we move on.

McCarthy is very human from day one. After a tough loss he jokes with the audience, "I thought about jumping out of the team plane on the way home."

He will often tell us, tongue-firmly-planted-in-cheek, "This [the show] is my favorite part of the day."

I see him when he's tired, when he's sick, when he's in a rush, and when he's relaxed and happy. He's a person. His parents come to nearly every home-game show in those first few years. They don't want to be recognized. They just want to sit in the front row and beam at their son. His daughter Alex comes to a show and I convince her to let us get one shot and introduce her. She's smiling in an embarrassed teenage way when the camera pans to her. The love McCarthy has for her is obvious.

I get to know McCarthy's parents better when we go to their home in Pittsburgh. The Packers are playing a preseason game in his hometown and we fly out a day early to meet up with Joe and Ellen McCarthy and do a story on his childhood home. But a huge rain storm is moving through and our plane is grounded for hours. When we finally do land, it's pouring and we're running late. I call the PR guy, who tells us to get there as fast as we can. We have to go directly to his parents' house instead of stopping at the hotel and getting some lunch. I'm eating almonds from the airport gift shop on the way and navigating.

The McCarthys live in a real working-class part of the city. The houses are stacked one right next to the other, with churches and corner grocery stores around them. Joe and Ellen are waiting for us, but the storm has knocked power out in the entire neighborhood and it's getting toward late afternoon and still raining. In other words, the lighting in the house is not good.

Another crew from a Green Bay station is already there, so we shoot some pictures the McCarthys have on display while we wait.

Because of the light, I have to interview Joe outside and Ellen in the entrance area, utilizing what little ambient light we have. There is a baby picture of Mike on the table in the front hallway and Ellen picks it up.

"It took him a while to sleep through the night. He still wanted that 3:00 a.m. feeding," she says with a laugh. There is nostalgia in her voice.

Ellen walks us around the house pointing out various things: pictures of Mike's daughter Alex, a Packers media guide with her son's face on it on the table in the living room, an autographed football, a framed shot of the whole family at Lambeau, and a Packers helmet magnet on their refrigerator. The house is small but very pleasant, like a favorite grandma's.

"You just feel so overwhelmed with the pride. I'm so proud of how he carries himself. He's stayed the same person. He's a good boy," she says, her eyes glistening, then quickly she corrects the last word with a slightly embarrassed laugh. "A good man."

"He was actually born over there," says Joe, pointing to a similar-looking house across the street. "But we moved here later."

Joe was a firefighter and police officer and tended bar nearby. He tells us how Mike would clean the bar as a teenager. He talks about how they all followed the Steelers and how Mike played basketball at a nearby Catholic school.

"He played all the sports," he recalls. "As far as him becoming head coach in football, I never thought that was coming. I think it must hit me every time I go to a game; then I realize Mike's the head coach here. I always feel excited for him."

"Did you see any leadership qualities in him early on?" I inquire as we stand on the front lawn during a brief break in the precipitation.

"He had his brother to boss around! And not to beat our own drum, but I'm sure he saw us: we're positive people, working all the time."

Joe is silver-haired with glasses and looks like the Irish father and grandfather that he is. He's wearing a white polo shirt. He has a direct way of talking and looking at you, sometimes pausing an extra beat to consider your words before he answers. Ellen is petite and speaks softly, so softly I sometimes have to strain to hear her. She has short, wavy, light brown hair done in a modern style, as if she's just emerged from the corner beauty salon. She wears little makeup and dresses in a comfortable way. Whenever I see her she has on khaki slacks and a simple top. She could easily be anyone's precious mother or grandmother.

I ask Ellen, "How do you think he'll handle the pressure of being the Packers coach?"

"You worry about the negatives, how he will handle them, but I think he's done very, very well with everything. I think he can handle it," she says. "He said [Green Bay] is just like home. He loves it there. It's a real good fit for him."

Ellen has a selection of muffins out on the table and offers us some. The late-afternoon light is really getting low now. We stand in their dining room overlooking the tiny backyard and chat. They have another son who is a lawyer in Pittsburgh and three daughters and they want me to know that they are proud of all of their children. In fact, they're having the entire clan over in honor of Mike being back in town.

"What are you serving?" I ask.

"Rigatoni, Pittsburgh barbecue, potato salad, chicken, and maybe some of Michael's favorite pizza," Ellen says, then quickly reminds herself, "Oh, wait, that was going to be a surprise!"

"Don't worry—he won't see this story," I say with a laugh, and she smiles, relieved.

As the time draws to a close I ask them, "Are you going to stay here tonight with no power?"

"Mike offered to put us up in a swanky hotel," says Joe. "But we told him no thanks. This is our home. We don't need a hotel in Pittsburgh. Plus, we've got flashlights and candles. It's not like we haven't been through power outages before."

They are good, solid people, I decide, as we say good-bye and head out. McCarthy clearly comes from a family that gave him an excellent and unpretentious upbringing.

Photographer Mark and I have to find the NBC affiliate station and our hotel, but we keep getting lost with the river and various bridges going this way and that. It starts pouring again. I call the station several times and ask for directions.

"Just tell me which side of the water you're on," I say. "Are you on the same side as Three Rivers Stadium?" I swear she tells me two different things and we're totally lost.

I'm trying to navigate Mark in the dark when my cell phone rings. It's one of my good friends from Milwaukee who wants to tell me about a medical problem her son is having. Now I'm desperately trying to hear her out and be sympathetic and helpful, while wandering from one riverbank to another and telling Mark, "No, I think we turn left here. No wait, right." Somehow we finally find the station, and later, after being fairly sure we're on the right side of the river, we make it to the hotel and check in. Once I settle into my room, I call Mark and tell him to come on up. We need to "track the piece," meaning he needs to record my voice track into his camera and give me the tape for editing.

The next day we meet up with McCarthy's lawyer brother, Joe Jr., who looks like a younger, slimmer version of Mike. During his lunch break he comes to the team hotel to do the interview in our photographer's hotel room because we have no other place with a decent background. We pull the curtains shut to block out the sunshine and rearrange some chairs in Mark's room.

"It was probably a typical older brother/younger brother relationship. Of course there were times we didn't agree on things," Joe Jr. says. The McCarthy brothers are four years apart, with Mike being older. "I was probably the more cerebral one. We didn't have a lot of fights or physical encounters because we knew how that would turn out. I learned from a very young age how to handle that.

"There's a great amount of pride and admiration that I have for Mike," he continues. "To be the head coach of the Green Bay Packers— there are very few opportunities that come along in a lifetime like that. One of the prize franchises, if not *the* prize franchise of the NFL. For Mike to be captain of the ship speaks for itself."

After the interview, Joe Jr. wants to know how things went with his parents.

"You can come up to my room and take a look on the editing machine if you want," I tell him. I had stayed up late the night before putting the piece together after Mark left me with the voice track. So we all troop up to my cramped room and watch.

"Wow, I can't believe you can edit right here in the hotel room," he says. The editing machine is a small, foldable item that looks like a suitcase. He seems pleased with what his parents told us and showed us at their house. Afterward we stroll with him outside through Pittsburgh's downtown and chat a little while getting some "b-roll" (video of him walking).

McCarthy's family will pop up in the audience at the show several times over the years. Sometimes a cousin or a friend of the family will be there, too. One year for Christmas Ellen summons me over. She bought me a gift: a selection of fancy lotions.

"Oh, my gosh, that is so thoughtful of you," I say and I really mean it.

Just a little into his time as coach, McCarthy meets a woman in Green Bay, Jessica. One night they are at a Marquette basketball game in Milwaukee and I'm sent to interview them. Jessica is tall and blond and looks like a California model. McCarthy is wearing a black leather jacket and jeans and has his arm around her. She has a similar outfit on, with high-heeled boots and her long hair pulled into a ponytail.

"Meet Jessica," McCarthy says to me.

"Hi, I like your name," she says as she smiles and we shake hands. I can tell McCarthy is smitten just by the way he looks at her in that tiny moment. I am not one bit surprised when they get married or when he tells us she's pregnant.

When baby Gabrielle is born I ask McCarthy if he can bring Jessica and the new baby to a show taping one time. Gabrielle is about three months old the day they do come after a win over Detroit. Jessica sits off to the side, holding and rocking Gabrielle, with her young nanny next to her.

Jessica McCarthy will send me Christmas cards for years. She has two sons from a previous marriage, and their family keeps growing when a second daughter, Isabella, comes along. One thing I am always impressed by is that Jessica puts their return address on the Christmas cards. I guess most of the Green Bay reporters probably know where they live anyway, but I don't, and this gesture is quaint and trusting, in a small-town way.

One year we have McCarthy's boss, Ted Thompson, on *The Mike McCarthy Show* as a guest and I am asking him question after question about the tight end situation, their draft needs, and more. Thompson is notorious for short answers, but he patiently responds to everything I am asking. In fact, I enjoy Thompson's clipped and direct style, so I'm surprised when one of the show's crew members gets on my case afterward.

"When you saw he wasn't going to answer those questions why did you keep on him?" he asks.

"That's the way he is. He always talks like that," I respond. It's also a little ironic that the woman who is sometimes told she doesn't ask enough about football is now being chastised for peppering the GM with football questions. Sigh.

Over the years McCarthy treats me like any other reporter and will joke around with Larry and me both on the air and during the commercial breaks. One week he's giving me a particularly hard time, saying something like, "Look out for this one. She'll bring the zinger questions." During the break we are sitting on stools and a woman in the front row compliments me on the skirt I'm wearing. It's got lace and sparkles and a depiction of Paris across the front.

"Where did you get that? It's beautiful," she says.

"Oh, thanks, Coach loaned it to me," I deadpan. The audience explodes with laughter. McCarthy laughs, too, and I tell him, "Hey, I had to get you back somehow."

But that night at home I wonder if maybe I went too far in being comfortable and casual with the coach. Maybe it would have been better to say, "Larry loaned it to me." I fret about this for a week, waiting to see if McCarthy will treat me coldly. He doesn't.

Wardrobe was always a challenge on the show. Our news director preached color—bright looks better than brown or black on television. People would actually call to complain if I wore purple (Vikings) or the colors of that week's opponent (say, silver and blue if the Packers were facing the Cowboys). I always felt that sporting green or yellow might take me away from the objectivity we were supposed to have, so that erased two colors from the mix. Silly? Perhaps, but what to wear was a weekly discussion I had with myself while looking through the closet. I also discovered early on that any skirt that wasn't down practically to my ankles looked terrible on TV. I have always had larger legs and when we had to sit on high stools in front of the audience, I thought my legs resembled sausages. So what was a girl to do? I wore a lot of pants and red or pink blazers!

I will do two stories with McCarthy that particularly stand out: "A Day in the Life of Mike McCarthy" and a personal tour of his office. I spent about a year requesting the "Day in the Life" piece and was turned down or pushed back several times. But part of the art of securing an interview is sometimes being willing to say, "I understand. Please let me know if this ever does fit into his schedule. I can make anytime work." Then e-mailing them again a few months later.

The Packers PR chief called me one summer day.

"OK, here's the deal. We have it all planned out," he says. "First you will come to his office at 7 a.m., where I have a daily briefing with him. Then he'll go to practice and he's willing to wear a microphone for a few minutes for you. Then we'll get you into the team meeting and the offensive meeting, but just for a little bit—like five minutes or less— each time for a photo op. Then there's a night practice. Does that sound good to you?"

"Are you kidding? It sounds great. See you at 7 a.m.," is my reply. I'm thrilled that patience paid off and we'll be getting unprecedented access to the head coach.

The story is fascinating to me, starting with that briefing meeting. The PR guy sits with McCarthy every single morning and tells him what the headlines of the day are—who is saying what in what newspaper and how they should respond to different things.

"OK, so [Player X] passed his physical in the Hutson Center this morning and has been cleared to play. You're going to get asked after practice today: how'd he look?" he says, going through his thick pile of notes. McCarthy nods, taking it all in over a cup of coffee as the morning sunlight is just starting to fill his office.

Then it's on to the 9:00 a.m. practice. McCarthy puts on the wireless microphone and is barking orders that sound like gibberish to me. Although not an actual play he calls, he might as well be yelling "007 singing cats ear noodle 38 north by northwest zipper salad 55" as players scramble into position. It's training camp and the stands around the field are packed with Packers fans. McCarthy has a laminated play sheet in his hand and keeps referring to it.

After ten minutes or so of McCarthy wearing the microphone, the PR guy goes to the field to retrieve it. Now we are allowed to shoot from the sidelines without getting any of that exclusive audio. Practice goes on for hours. We are not permitted into the lunch area, so photographer Joe and I get sub sandwiches and wait in the car for the next round of meetings.

This is one of the first times a camera has been let into the massive team meeting room. All of the players are there, wearing sweatpants and sitting casually in the classroom-style seats. It's like a large college lecture hall with a projector and PowerPoint at the front and auditorium-style seating going up at least thirty rows. There are also team pictures of all the Packers Super Bowl championship years. McCarthy stands at the front in his green Packers sweatshirt. There is a night practice that evening at a local high school. It's the old site of City Stadium, where the first Packers played, so they are doing this as a nod to history and to give the fans something different. The part of the meeting we are allowed to shoot is McCarthy going over the schedule for the day: snacks, treatments, and meetings. He also runs through basic details of that practice, using the PowerPoint to show a diagram of City Stadium and exactly where different drills will take place. Then he turns the floor over to a member of his staff, who breaks down game statistics for the Packers. On this day he's going over some new rules with a game education video. He shows them film detailing certain infractions and why they're being called. Once again we're allowed only a few minutes to give viewers the general feel of the meeting. Then we're ushered out so they have some privacy.

McCarthy is also scheduled to have a meeting with Brian Baldinger, a former NFL player who is in town to broadcast that weekend's preseason game. For this, McCarthy and Baldinger sit by the sunny windows back in the coach's office and talk and laugh loudly in a jocular way. A quick shot and we wait for the next thing.

The offensive coaches are all meeting in one of their rooms. It's a white-walled, bright and sunny space with a large conference table and a projector on the wall. They all have huge three-ring binders with them and are listening as McCarthy and offensive coordinator Joe Philbin go over the practice plan for that night. The PR staff has told us we cannot use any audio other than the low hum of voices. In other words, we can't divulge any of their plan on the air. Understandable. I really have no problem with it as they are being more than accommodating by giving us inside access.

We head over to the stadium to wait for the team busses for the night practice. I have to start logging and editing because the piece is scheduled to air the next night. Then there is another two-hour practice followed by the return of the busses to Lambeau. By now it's getting toward 10 p.m. I had hoped to end the piece with McCarthy back in his office, but the PR guy has not told me yet if this is possible, so Joe and I sit in the car again in the parking lot. We're both exhausted. How does McCarthy put in these kinds of hours all day, every day?

Around 10:30, Joe and I decide to pull up stakes. We still have a two-hour drive back to Milwaukee ahead of us and we're feeling that we're never going to be given clearance to go to McCarthy's office. He must be done for the day. We pull out of the parking lot and stop at the gas station across the street when my cell phone rings and it's the PR guy telling me that McCarthy is ready for us. Well, how can I turn that down? Dragging our tired bodies back to Lambeau and up the dark stairs we see him at his desk, the lamp on as he looks over notes from the day.

"Wow, I'm tired from one day of following you. I can't believe the hours you put in," I tell him.

"That's training camp in the National Football League. That's the way it goes," he says. We're allowed to get a few more shots and ask him a closing question or two.

"Do you thrive on schedules like this? Are you the type of person who enjoys being constantly on the go?"

"I think it's important not to waste time. In this business there's nothing worse than downtime, wasted time."

To illustrate his point he shows me the next day's schedule laid out on a spreadsheet with every activity shaded a different color. It's packed top to bottom in greens, yellows, reds, and purples. I don't see an open white spot anywhere.

It's time to say good night. We're practically punch-drunk driving home to Milwaukee at 1:00 a.m.

The piece airs in our 10:00 newscast the next night and also during halftime of a preseason game. It will win an award for best sports story that year from the Milwaukee Press Club. But I like the story I do a few years later even more because it shows him as a father.

This time I have requested a tour of his office, and after a little more nudging and being patient with the PR people, I am finally granted permission. He will give me a half hour of his time during training camp, which I appreciate because I really do know how busy these coaches are.

That morning we tape *The Mike McCarthy Show* and afterward I say to him, "Are you still OK with us coming up to your office at lunchtime?"

"I was never OK with it, but I'm doing it," he says with a laugh. Sometimes coaches are persuaded to do these things by PR.

"I like a little honesty," I tell him.

The tour starts in the outer office occupied by his secretary. Then he walks us through the door to his personal space.

"It's my understanding that this is the same doorframe Coach Lombardi had in his office," McCarthy says. "It was part of the renovation project. It's kind of neat to walk through that every day."

We turn toward the wall on the left, which is covered in brightly colored portraits of Jessica and his children.

"It's an active, lively, diverse household," he says, his eyes sparkling as he pans across each one.

"Do you sometimes look at this wall if you need to be grounded, need to take a moment to reflect or de-stress?" I ask him.

"I look at them all the time. I think it's important to spend time each day in thought. My time is early in the morning and late at night, when I'm not running from here to there."

His wooden desk sits in the middle of the room facing a bank of windows. Behind the desk he displays a series of personal and professional mementos. There's a Wheaties box with a picture of the team, some trophies, and a folded American flag.

"That was the flag that flew over Lambeau at my first game. Bob Harlan gave it to me," he says.

There is also, curiously, a Big Bird stuffed animal. His explanation, "It's kind of a personal item between my wife and me. The irony of it is our daughter, Gabrielle, she has a Big Bird that kind of runs the house. She carries Big Bird everywhere. She calls it BB."

On his desk sits a picture of him and Jessica looking wind-swept on a boat near their Texas vacation home and a paperweight that says "Honey" on it.

"A gift from Jessica?" I ask.

"I would think that would be from Jessica, yes," he says with a laugh.

There's a picture of Gabrielle as a baby, her eyes closed in blissful sleep.

"She's a McCarthy; she can sleep anywhere," he notes.

"Can you sleep anywhere?"

"I used to be able to. I think this job has taken that trait away from me." He is in a relaxed mood.

Next to the desk is a smoothie machine and a spot to make his favorite drink: green tea. He tells me the smoothie machine was a Christmas gift from some of the assistant coaches. A CD player waits patiently to be used. He listens every morning to a mix of country and soft rock. His current favorite? He describes the band as "a little like the early Lynyrd Skynyrd."

There is also a blow-up punching bag in a referee shirt with the name "Pereira" on the back.

"Who's this guy?"

"Mike Pereira was the director of officials. He gave all the coaches this punching bag at the owners' meeting one year and our equipment manager, Red Batty, added his name to the back. The boys [McCarthy's stepsons] love it when they come here. They just beat the hell out of it. I have to settle them down."

Directly across from McCarthy's desk is a sitting area with a few small couches (all in green, of course), a bookshelf, and a TV.

"I think it's important to get out from behind the desk." And the books? A quick glance at the titles reveals *The Best Game Ever*, *That First Season*, and *Common Sense Success*.

"I used to read a lot when I was single. Not much time now . . . but I guess there will be plenty of time for that. . . ."

There is also a framed photo of McCarthy with daughter Alex at a NASCAR race.

"That was a good time we had together," he says with fatherly love and a smile.

We're just wrapping up the interview when we hear a small voice, like that of a toddler, coming from the outer office.

"Well, look who's here," says McCarthy as we walk out and see Gabrielle seated happily on the chair of McCarthy's secretary. She's about two years old and is nibbling on a plate of plain noodles and fruit that rests on a cafeteria tray, clearly from the Packers lunch area.

"Daddy! Daddy, *sit*!" she orders, pointing to the chair next to her.

"She's very bossy," he says with a chuckle, but of course he plops down next to her and snuggles a bit, encouraging her to eat more noodles. He tells us that Gabrielle is a regular lunchtime visitor. We get some really good video of the two of them interacting for a few moments. Gabrielle is pointing at things around the room and labeling everything: "Plant. Flower. Pret-ty."

McCarthy kisses her head and tells her he'll be right back. His secretary stays with Gabrielle as we head into an adjoining room, this one a meeting room with a giant table in the middle and wipe boards all around. The training camp depth chart is written on one wall, and both McCarthy and the PR guy make us promise not to show that on the air as it is a bit of privileged information showing who the coaches think are the top to bottom at each position.

There is also a sign on the wall reading, "Less volume, more creativity."

"I can't help but notice the sign," I tell him.

"That's kind of a mantra I've put on the coordinators the last couple of years," he says.

Back near Gabrielle, McCarthy feeds her strawberries. He says that these family moments mean everything to him, but it's time to get back to work.

He kneels down to her level.

"Say, 'Go Pack Go!'"

A huge smile spreads across her face.

We wrap up the interview and thank McCarthy. We have so much good stuff, I feel like I could write a ten-minute piece. It winds up being a little less than three minutes, which is still too long for our producer. She sends me a note telling me that the station's new motto is not to go longer than two minutes for *anything*. The viewers can't take in-depth pieces. They want snappy, or so she says. I write her back and say, "But it's Packers and it's exclusive." We're always told Packers are the A-number one thing in the market (next to weather and breaking news, of course). She harrumphs, but lets me slide it through.

The story also garners a giant picture in *Packer Plus*, a weekly newspaper devoted to a certain team. It is a cool shot of McCarthy in a personal moment with his daughter and the noodles.

I will host *The Mike McCarthy Show* for seven years, driving back and forth to Green Bay every Monday. During training camp he wants to tape at 7:30 a.m.—the only time of day he has any free space. During the season we tape at 4:00 p.m. The audience waxes and wanes between thirty people and two hundred, depending on the day, time, and whether or not the team is winning and people are excited. We have one group of about eight regulars that I am so thankful for because at least we know we'll have them come hell, bad weather, or a losing streak. They are all retirees who are absolutely crazed Packers fans. They come dressed head to toe in green and gold, with Packers earrings and purses as accessories. They get the front row every time because they always arrive hours early.

There is an eclectic mix of characters at each show, ranging from a grandma with a bright gold mohawk to a long-haired, shirt-open guy with a Packers guitar. We never know what questions the audience will ask McCarthy. Larry warms up the crowd each week and asks for volunteers, taking the first four or five hands. Often the questions relate directly to the game or to strategy ("Why don't you pass more on third down?"), but it's also interesting how many people just want a tiny glimpse into the coach's world. The most popular non-football questions seem to be, "What do you do in your free time?" and "What do you like best about being the head coach of the Green Bay Packers?"

I have to meet with that week's player guest in the green room before each show and chat with him for a few minutes before we go out to tape. The Packers pick this player after each week's game, the idea being that it's someone who has performed well. It's here, behind the scenes, that you get to see the players relaxed and also view them interacting with McCarthy for a short time. He often comes rolling in a few minutes late, still buttoning his coat. He is usually wearing casual, Buster Brown–type shoes and jokes with us that he's too busy to grab socks.

You can tell McCarthy has a good rapport with the players. He always asks them how they're feeling, usually even in a more specific way like, "How's that knee doing today?" and they all seem loose joking with him. Sometimes when he's really late, a player might say, "Well, that's a late fine for you, Coach," and he will just laugh and needle the guy right back. I'm guessing many NFL coaches don't have such a comfortable relationship with their players.

Some players bring their wives or girlfriends to watch the interview, sometimes their mothers or fathers. McCarthy always introduces himself, shakes hands, and asks them where they're from and how long they're in town. I also have lots of time to make small talk with the players. It's my job to figure out if there is some tidbit from the game that the player would like to discuss. I would like to bring something to the table that viewers haven't already seen, so I will often start off asking if there was a discussion or a play that stands out in the player's mind. It is here that I find out that Charles Woodson had a conversation with Morgan Burnett, telling him to watch out for something that did indeed happen, which led to an interception. John Kuhn tells us about Jared Allen of the Vikings and the funny things he has to say to his competitors. I also try to see if there is a bit of a personal story the player might want to tell on the show. Woodson has a young son and I ask him in the green room if Charles Jr. has said anything humorous lately in toddler-speak. Charles laughs and tells this story, which he then repeats on the air:

"My wife and I call each other 'babe' all the time . . . like, 'Babe, can you get me some orange juice?' So now our son will say, 'Can I have a snack . . . babe?'" The audience, clapping and laughing, clearly appreciates the glimpse into this star player's personal life.

Greg Jennings tells us in the green room that he was late because he was watching his three young girls while his wife went to a meeting, so on the air I say, "Greg, you're a very grounded person. Here you are, a superstar wide receiver, and why don't you tell the audience where you were right before the taping of this show?"

"I was at home, playing Barbies with my daughters," he says in his soft-spoken way with his million-dollar smile. He is wearing Packers sweatpants and a sweatshirt, and I can just picture him on the floor with the Barbie Dreamhouse. "I was Mr. Mom. My wife had to go with the other Super Bowl wives to a meeting. I love it, though. I love hanging out with my girls."

It's these personal tidbits, in my opinion, that many people will remember even more than why they went for it on fourth down.

When Aaron Rodgers is the guest, the audience size swells. Our floor director is so starstruck he can't help but bring his sixth-grade son back into the green room and ask Rodgers for a picture, to which Rodgers smiles and obliges.

"I never do this," says the floor director. "But we are such big fans of yours. Do you mind?"

"Sure, no problem."

Rodgers is affable in this behind-the-scenes situation, but also coolly aloof about anything personal. When I ask him how his Christmas was and what family members were there, he clams up, but it doesn't surprise me. Rodgers will never, ever say anything about his life off the field, including whether or not he's dating anyone, although he's been asked in many settings. I can understand how hard it is for a single superstar to trust anyone. At least Favre met Deanna before he was famous. I feel for Rodgers in this regard. A year later, in 2012, Rodgers is rumored to be engaged to a woman he knew from his hometown of Chico, California. Makes perfect sense, I think to myself—she's someone he has a history with and can trust, someone who knew him when he was just Aaron Rodgers, not AARON RODGERS.

On the air I ask Rodgers about his big-screen desires.

"We've seen you in a lot of commercials [the State Farm ads are all over the tube]. Any interest in movies or a guest spot on a television show?"

"Yes. I almost had a chance to be on *Entourage* last year, but the timing didn't work out. But, yes, I'd love to do that. Merlin Olsen had a lot of success in *Little House on the Prairie*. I could see doing something like that."

"On another note: I want to ask you about what's called photo bombing," I say. "Where you pop up in the background of every captains' picture? Is that your goal, to be in every single one?"

The captains' picture is taken right before each game and includes three Packers players who have been chosen to be captains that week. And of course it also includes Rodgers, the jokester.

"Yes. It started one week and it's kind of grown from there. Mike has all of the captains' pictures up on a wall and it's fun to see how it's evolved over the years—the different facial hair and things."

On the air we edit in captains' picture after captains' picture: there's Rodgers peeking around the corner in some of them, smack dab in the middle in others, and even looking through binoculars in one. We also pull some Merlin Olsen video off YouTube and put that in.

Rodgers will come on *The Mike McCarthy Show* once every year. During one of the first years, he invites his older brother, Luke, to come along. This is his first year as a starter and he's under a lot of pressure, so I ask him who his confidant is, whom he turns to in life.

"Well, he's sitting right over there," Rodgers says with a smile as he points at Luke. The camera cuts away to a lankier, longer-haired, more California-hippie version of Aaron.

"So, you two are very close as siblings?"

"Well. . . . Sometimes, anyway," he says and the audience laughs. I have seen Rodgers's parents in person only once. When the Packers played in San Francisco they drove from Chico and I got a brief introduction as they stood in the stands watching Aaron go through warm-ups. I asked the PR guy to ask them if we could interview them during the game. No. Could we get a shot of them watching from the stands? No. They did not want to be publicly acknowledged in any way. It's starting to make sense that the apple doesn't fall far from the tree. Aaron's privacy likely stems in part from theirs.

During the playoffs leading to Super Bowl XLV, I asked Rodgers in a group interview setting in the locker room if he felt bad for the injured Packers who could not take part in the run-up to the big game. His answer was interesting. He said he thought the injured guys should stay in Green Bay to rehab if they wanted to be more a part of the team. He added that he was proud that he always stuck around Green Bay for longer than needed in the offseason. This particular comment blew up just a few hours later when Jermichael Finley, Nick Barnett, and other injured players heard about it and started tweeting angrily, saying that Rodgers had no idea how hard it was to find rehab space at Lambeau with so many guys down and out.

Rodgers had to essentially apologize and backpedal, making amends with his teammates.

"Who asked him that question?" I saw on various chat boards. One reporter from a Milwaukee radio station came to my defense.

"It was Jessie Garcia, but she meant no malice," he said. "He just took it in the direction he took it in."

This reporter and I had actually gotten into a little tiff a few years prior, so I was grateful for the boost.

The disagreement came about when a Packers player was miffed with the radio station reporter for something he wrote on his blog. The reporter was trying to smooth things over with the player in the locker room. I didn't know this. I saw the reporter talking with the guy by his locker and I went over to ask the player a question. I waited what I thought was a respectful distance away for the reporter to finish and then stepped up to ask the player what I needed, but the reporter cornered me afterward.

"Thanks a lot. Didn't you see I was talking privately with [Player X]?" he asked. "I would not have done that to you."

"I didn't know it was private. I apologize."

The next day a friend told me that the reporter was talking about me on the radio. I tuned in just in time to hear him say that a female Milwaukee reporter had violated locker room etiquette by crowding him during his alone time with the player. I was kind of shocked because I thought this had been put to bed the day before. I e-mailed the guy explaining my side and he wrote back his side and admitted he never should have taken it to the airwaves. This sort of thing can happen in a locker room filled with reporters from competing media outlets. There are some unspoken rules about etiquette (no autographs is another), but I had not realized I had broken the one about allowing a fellow journalist ample one-on-one time. The Wisconsin media in general is pretty gentle with each other—even friendly—but there are moments of annoyance or talking behind someone's back. Then there are times when we do stand up and support each other and that's how I felt about the incident surrounding my interview of Rodgers.

Of all of my memories of *The Mike McCarthy Show*, one really stands out. My husband, kids, and I had gone to Minneapolis for Christmas week to see Paul's family. We were scheduled to tape a show on Christmas Eve day, so I had to fly the night of December 23 from Minneapolis to Green Bay and sleep over for a 9 a.m. taping. How an airline can lose your luggage on a short, direct flight like that baffles me, but I got to

Green Bay (late because of bad weather) and stood with dozens of other passengers like lonely puppy dogs at the baggage carousel watching it go round and round without any trace of our stuff. Finally, we all kind of looked at each other, heaved a collective deep sigh, and went to find the baggage office. It was already about midnight and the one person working there was completely overwhelmed. He said he'd try to look into it but nothing would get resolved that night. I went to the hotel without anything to wear on the air eight hours later. I had no toothbrush, no deodorant, no shampoo, no nothing.

I lay down and tried to sleep—in my clothes (no pj's either)—after getting a toothbrush from the front desk. I couldn't relax and maybe got two hours of shut-eye. The next morning was Christmas Eve.

I had to meet the rest of the crew at the taping, which meant taking a cab from the hotel to Lambeau Field.

"Good morning, Merry Christmas," said my cab driver, a Native American woman.

"Merry Christmas. This may sound a bit unusual, but could we stop at Target? I'll have you keep the meter running while I run in for a few things I need."

"Oh, sure, hon, no problem."

So I dashed into Target with the warm cab waiting in the bitter morning. Inside the store I was like a crazed person looking this way and that. Eyeliner, foundation, a little blush. Some black pants; here's a black silky shirt with a little design on it that will do. No time to try it on—just buy it and hope for the best. When I finally got to the show the crew said happily, "Hey, how are you? What's new?"

"You have no idea how much I've been through in the last twelve hours just to be here!"

McCarthy strolled in looking happy and relaxed; I still felt like a mess, but we got through the show and I took a cab to the airport to fly back to Minneapolis and reunite with the family. That night we were staying at Paul's sister's house, in her converted attic space. I put Charlie to bed and fell asleep next to him at 8:30, exhausted beyond belief. It took a whole week before the airline located my luggage. Somehow it had been put on a bus to Appleton. I had to swing by the airport the next time I was in Green Bay to get it.

I also had many experiences on icy roads during those *Mike McCarthy Show* years. Anything can happen while driving in Wisconsin in winter. I got used to it—leaving a little early when I could and occasionally throwing an overnight bag in the backseat, just in case, which came in handy more than once. One night after a show I tried to get home but made it only about twenty minutes out of Green Bay, where the roads were as bad as I've ever seen them. Traffic was crawling at twenty miles per hour and cars were spun out all along the way. I gripped the wheel, but the whole experience was made worse by blowing snow that reduced visibility to almost zero. This is crazy, I thought. I wanted to get home and see the kids, but I wanted to be alive more than anything, so I pulled off and found a hotel, collapsing on the bed with pent-up anxiety. Even the next day the roads were bad, but at least the snow had stopped. My family hated these weekly trips and worried a lot.

"Is this really worth it?" my mom asked me at least a few times a year.

"I signed up for the job. I need to make every effort to be there, but I won't be stupid," I told her.

Near the end of my time with *The Mike McCarthy Show* I was having neck problems. It started when I went to the chiropractor for a routine neck adjustment. I'd had them before with no issues. My neck was feeling really sore, so I made an appointment and he did his usual crack. The next day was a day off from school for the boys and we took the train to Chicago. It was a great, fun day filled with the Field Museum and Michigan Avenue, but I had a bad headache all day. I didn't mention it to anyone. We seemed too busy to stop at a Walgreens. I just powered on, but on the train on the way home I rubbed and rubbed my neck, trying to get rid of the headache.

The next day I had to take Charlie to the dentist. On the way I started to feel really off. I was dizzy and nauseated and my eyes seemed unable to focus fully on the road. It was incredibly scary, especially when my left arm went numb in the dentist's waiting room. Oh, please, don't let me have a stroke or a seizure right here while Charlie is getting his teeth cleaned.

I stepped outside and called my mom, telling her I was feeling odd. Somehow I managed to drive us home, but it was a terrible fifteen minutes. I'm sure now that I was also having a panic attack brought on by the symptoms. At home I called my doctor who told me to go immediately to the emergency room.

"You have stroke symptoms. Get there now."

Two MRIs, a CT scan, an x-ray, and an overnight hospitalization later, I was discharged and diagnosed with bone spurs in my neck causing a pinched nerve that some doctors thought was exacerbated by the chiropractic adjustment. The left side of my neck proceeded to hurt for the next few months, and I also had spells of feeling dizzy or flushed or just plain off, but I still had to do the show. It was torturous for a while. Finally, I decided to tell McCarthy and Larry that I was having trouble turning my head to the left—it made everything worse. They were extremely accommodating and offered to switch seats around so I wouldn't have to look left so often. I did several shows with a small heating pad taped to the back of my neck and a few others with a small ice pack. I don't think anyone noticed as my hair usually covered it.

Our last show of the year—and my last show as host, period—came after the Packers lost in shocking fashion at home to the Giants (again!) in January 2012. The Packers had gone 15–1 in the season and everyone expected they would be Super Bowl bound. They had home-field advantage, so it would be no problem, right? But the Packers played a laissez-faire, sloppy game, and it was Eli Manning and the Giants who looked like the motivated bunch. Packers fans filed out of the stadium, stunned. Two days later I had to go over this loss with the coach.

The Packers had decided there would be no audience for this show. It having been a terrible loss, all they wanted was to keep the show as streamlined as possible for the coach. So it was just me, Larry, and McCarthy, who seemed to be in a decent mood despite his disappointment. He actually seemed to want to talk; maybe it was therapeutic. We asked him about the turnovers, the dropped balls, and whether or not he should have rested Rodgers in the final game of the regular season to keep him fresh for the play-offs.

As we wrapped up, I looked around the empty atrium. It would have been buzzing with activity if they were getting ready for the NFC championship. Instead, there were about three people lounging in the sports bar. But despite the loss, and his head swirling with other things,

The last day of *The Mike McCarthy Show*, following the 2011 season. We all had been thinking Super Bowl, but a 15-1 record in the regular season turned out not to be enough. Despite the loss, the coach was in relatively good spirits. As for me, my neck was hurting; I had a hand warmer taped to the back of it. I told McCarthy after the show that it was my last year hosting and he gave me a hug and said, "You've been great." I told him he was a pleasure to work with.

McCarthy still gave me a hug and said, "Take care of that neck," as he headed off with the PR guy toward the elevators. I thought back to his parents and realized you can trace good people to their roots and the McCarthys were *good* people.

THE TEAM PLANE

NORMALLY REPORTERS DO NOT FLY on the team plane. We have to go through multiple airports, dragging our luggage and hearing the same safety spiel a thousand times. Thank you very much, Delta/American/United flight attendants. It's the pure act of traveling all the time that wears down many a reporter while knowing the team is jetting through the air first class all the way.

I did have one chance to fly on the Packers plane. It came in 2007 after a preseason game in Nashville. We had to tape a *Mike McCarthy Show* early the next day and we didn't think I'd get back on time if we didn't work something out with the team. I called the travel secretary and explained the situation. Before granting me permission, he had to run it up the flagpole to the team president and GM. They are *very* particular about whom they let on the plane—for both security reasons and privacy. I understood, but I also held my breath. If they didn't let me on I would have to try to hop a 5:00 a.m. flight out of Nashville to Milwaukee and then to Green Bay and be a complete wreck come show time.

"OK, you're in," the secretary got back to me. Whew. I still had to fly commercial on the way down, but I would be on the charter on the way back.

After the game, I was told to report to the busses waiting for the team in the loading-dock area of the Titans stadium. These were your standard Greyhound-type busses, three or four of them with placards on the front window: "Staff," "Coaches and Players." I was instructed to go to the staff bus only. I sat down across from Sarah Quick, one of the nicest PR people in the NFL.

"Do you want something to eat? They have pizza and sandwiches," she said.

"Oh, thanks, I'm OK for now."

I was feeling a lot of adrenaline—it was only a bus, but it seemed cool, exciting. I tried to keep my blood from pumping too fast while we waited, and waited, for the busses to fill up. It took quite a while as they loaded equipment into the underbelly.

Finally we started rolling, and when you have a police escort you can really roll. A couple of squad cars led the parade while others raced ahead and created a roadblock at every intersection. I felt like a rock star as we motored past curious onlookers, some of them waving and jumping around, onto the highway, and then zoomed across town to the airport in record time. Once there, we had to stop at a security check-point that led directly to the tarmac. This took another little while as security talked with the bus driver and must have called for clearance.

Eventually the busses pulled up to a stop and we all unloaded and walked directly up a ramp into a makeshift security area—and I say *makeshift* because it was nothing like what normal people have to go through. They had several tables set up to make the lines go faster. We each had to put our bag on the table and they opened the cover and took a peek inside. When it was my time I was grateful I had remembered not to put anything embarrassing at the top, especially because a defensive back was right behind me in line. Security put each bag through a metal detector, and then we were sent right down the ramp to the waiting plane. All along the wall of the ramp was a long food table—piled with more pizza, fruit, granola bars, and lots of drink choices. The flight attendants stood at the bottom of the ramp, and they were all wearing

Packers T-shirts with green and gold earrings and beads around their necks. They seemed to know a lot of players and coaches, and there was an easy, joking feel in the air. I grabbed an apple and stepped onto the plane. The first person I saw was McCarthy. He was turned the other way, laughing about something with a few of the assistant coaches. In that one moment I could see he was more relaxed than I had hardly ever seen him in public. He turned toward me and did a double take.

"You're on this flight?" He was smiling but seemed genuinely surprised. Apparently running it up the flagpole did not include him.

"Yeah, I have to get back for the show tomorrow," I explained.

"I guess they let anyone on these days, huh?" he responded with a chuckle, turning back to the assistant coaches and continuing to rib them about some inside joke.

Each seat on the plane was already designated with a name card. It was a huge plane, with extra-wide seats and enough of them so that everyone had an empty spot between them and the next person in the row. Coaches appeared to be in first class, with staff members in the middle and players at the back. My seat was next to the radio engineer who makes sure the broadcast goes out cleanly across the airwaves each game. I settled back and tried to relax but found I was still feeling jacked up. You're on the Packers team plane, I told myself, but don't freak about it. Relax. I pulled out my notebook and started trying to work on the next day's show. Things got quiet awfully quickly on the plane as the jovial joking was replaced by it's-late-and-we're-tired silence. The attendants did not do the usual security speech. I figured some of the larger players probably weren't wearing seat belts anyway.

Right after takeoff they served a full dinner. The cabin lights dimmed and I don't think I heard a murmur from anyone in the back. Brett Favre was still on the team, and I was trying to picture him, sprawled in his seat or listening to headphones. If we crash, I will go down in history as having died with the Packers, I thought, then pushed that away. The weather is good and the Packers must employ good pilots, right? We'll make it back. And we did. Something that would have taken me at least six hours to accomplish in the civilian world was over in less than two hours. As we came into Green Bay, I looked down at the lights below. Such a small town—that's really made clear when you fly in on a Sunday night and know that everyone below you is sound asleep, resting up for work and school the next day. I remembered stories I had heard of how people sometimes left their house lights on as a welcome home to the Packers plane. I felt emotional and proud of my home state. I loved that the Packers have an open-air stadium when other cities went for the sterile, closed-in look; I loved the whole stockholders aspect of the team. The Packers are a treasure, I thought to myself, and I was happy to get to play a small part in broadcasting their games.

It was very late when we landed, and the thing about coming into Austin Straubel airport at 1:00 a.m. is that it is absolutely dead. We walked off the plane, past a couple of bored-looking security guys, and outside into the dark parking lot. Austin Straubel has no shuttle busses, no remote parking. Some Walmarts are bigger than Austin Straubel. Everyone's car was right there. Several players said hello to tired-looking wives or girlfriends picking them up in Escalades. A few players still had ice packs taped to various parts of their bodies as they eased their way into the vehicles. There were no autograph seekers; there was nothing at all. As for me, I was staying at the Radisson across the road. I could have walked there but I didn't think that was the best idea in the middle of the night, so I asked Larry McCarren if he could drop me off. We hopped into his red pickup truck for the thirty-second drive. Well, that was cool, I thought to myself. But now it's time to sleep. I had a show to do the next day. My one big shot at the team plane was over, but it was definitely an experience of a lifetime.

THE TEAM BUS

THE PACKERS HAVE a Tailgate Tour every spring. They drive around the state in a bright green and gold bus, while holding pep rally–type events for five straight days. In May 2012 I was assigned to cover four of the team's stops and, while I knew it would be fun, I also found it to be a surprisingly moving experience, seeing the love of the people gush like an open fire hydrant. Yes, they're "just a football team," but in Wisconsin it's more than that: they bring us together with a common reason to cheer. My mother calls this a tribal mentality that is missing in modern society. We need to be able to bond with each other in a collective way. We desire some form of release from stress and bad news. Supporting our local teams gives us something intriguing to talk about and just makes us feel united.

We started by meeting the team at an assisted living facility in Kenosha. The bus rolled into the tree-lined lot right on time. The elderly from the facility had all gathered near the front doors. Some had Packers shirts on, or green beads, some carried footballs and Sharpies. Many moved slowly with the aid of walkers; a few were in wheelchairs. When the behemoth Packers stepped off the bus, the group went crazy clapping and cheering.

"Can I hug you?" a female resident asked William Henderson.

"I will always take a hug from a pretty lady," he answered—the perfect thing to say. She beamed as he wrapped his mighty arms around her frail frame. The Packers were shaking hands, talking, and giving high fives to everyone within reach. The Tailgate Tour that year consisted of Henderson; current players Jordy Nelson and Mason Crosby; former players Charlie Peprah, Marco Rivera, my show cohost Larry McCarren; and Packers president and CEO Mark Murphy. They proceeded to spend the next forty-five minutes in the dining area signing autographs and joking with one older person after another. There was even a postal carrier there, still in her full uniform, standing in line for autographs. I got the sense she somehow found out the Packers were coming and scooted over after her shift.

One resident, wearing a Packers baseball cap, took a break from talking with the players to lean on his walker and reflect. "I'm an ex-educator from Kenosha. I was a principal and assistant superintendent," he told us. "It's nice to see that they're here and I had a ball autographed by a bunch of them. [The residents] are really excited. You can see it."

Then it was on to the Boys & Girls Club of Kenosha. They were expecting a crowd of seven hundred, and a giant room, as big as an airplane hangar, was set up with rows and rows of chairs and a stage. Vendors with Packers gear were unpacking items at nearby tables, and a band played in the corner. The Packers first had dinner with some of the kids and then went into a back-room sports area to throw footballs on the club's indoor Astroturf field.

"Who's played football before?" Henderson asked as young hands shot up. He started tossing them a blue football.

"You guys have been practicing, haven't you?" Nelson said with a chuckle while catching zingers from a group in another corner.

"Ready, set, go," barked McCarren, making them run out routes.

Even Murphy stood in a circle, flipping the ball back and forth with five kids. He would try to fool them by looking one way and throwing it the other, or whipping it behind his back.

"Good catch!" Murphy encouraged a girl as she bobbled one of his no-look passes before holding on.

"[The coolest part] was meeting them in real life instead of watching them on TV," a boy of about ten told us.

The team later took the stage to a rock-star reception, each player escorted by a group of kids and introduced to wild applause. The Packers patiently answered questions and ended by throwing mini footballs into a crowd of waving arms. Little kids were perched on their dads' shoulders shouting, "Here, here!" But the Packers weren't done yet. They all sat at long white tables to sign autographs, and it seemed nearly all of the seven hundred people had paid the extra dollars for autographs. The line backed up all the way around the room. All of the money raised went right back to the Boys & Girls Club. We interviewed a few Packers off to the side.

"I've had a blast," said Peprah. "It gave me the opportunity to see a lot of the state."

"It's a special thing that I don't think happens many other places," added Crosby. "We had a great talk at dinner last night. We were talking about how we love being a part of this organization and how it's different than a lot of other organizations. We talked to Charlie [Peprah] a lot about it; he's obviously been different places, and Marco was in Dallas. Just the bond we've been able to form with former players. Once you're a Packer, you're always a Packer—those are the kinds of things we were talking about."

The next morning I was back on the Packers bus beat. They had already mingled with diners at a restaurant in Kenosha when we caught up with them at Riverside University High School in Milwaukee, a diverse urban school. It was planned as a surprise for the freshmen and sophomores, who were told only that they would be attending an assembly. The bus pulled up outside as some school officials went to usher the team in. The players entered the auditorium from the back to audible gasps. The crowd crackled with wonder as the current and former players, all dressed in their jerseys, went down the aisles and stepped onto the stage. The Packers spent more than thirty minutes delivering a message of responsibility, telling the kids about not bullying and being smart in life.

"Every single decision you make will affect you sooner or later," Peprah emphatically said into his microphone as he paced the stage.

The kids sat in rapt attention. The Packers brought T-shirts this time and pitched them to the crowd at the end.

"Tell me one thing you learned today," I asked one boy who caught a shirt.

"That the Packers are just like everyone else. [They were] just students like everyone else that were getting bullied," he replied.

The team had offered to let us ride with them from this stop to the next one—about a twenty-minute jaunt up the highway to an elementary school. As they left Riverside, we walked outside and got onto the bus. I was curious to see how they had it set up. These guys were doing four or five appearances a day and driving from one corner of the state to the next, all across Wisconsin. The bus did not disappoint. Oversized recliner-type seats and small sofas lined each side, with card tables, a bathroom, and a well-stocked kitchenette toward the back. It was all decorated in dark blue and maroon tones with pleated blue blinds on the big windows. There was a big-screen TV mounted over the driver's head with several smaller TVs set up at convenient intervals. The players were already settled in their seats.

"I hope you don't mind. We're crashing your bus," I said.

"Come on in!" replied Peprah with his usual big grin. I had never seen him in a bad mood.

The principal from Riverside stepped onto the bus right before we took off. He wanted to thank the players and also tell them a few things about his school. He recited a very impressive graduation rate, waved, and stepped off. We started rolling away and some of the players turned to each other and to me.

"Wow, what he was saying—that was really impressive," marveled Crosby. "What a cool high school."

We all nodded in agreement.

I had made the decision to ask a player to give us a tour of the bus. It would be a lot more interesting coming from one of them than from me. I had the perfect person in mind: Henderson. I remembered him from his playing days and knew he would give a great tour. I was right. We handed him our microphone and let him go at it.

"We have state-of-the-art everything. Great players as well as great electronics," he said, gesturing with his hands as he talked and the camera panned around. "All the wireless options, we've got TV, video. If you go to the back of the bus, it's set up with the condiment section. It's even got a nice, handy handle for us to use as we walk so we don't fall down. The Packers do everything top-notch."

He stopped and asked each player a few questions about their experiences on the tour.

Peprah: "I've been talking [to the kids] about making the right decisions. We know at this age the right decisions are not necessarily the most popular. Hopefully I can encourage them to think twice about making wrong decisions and influence them to have better decision making."

Crosby: "Something that really moved me was going to the children's hospital [in Madison]. We could have spent the whole day there. Just walking around, trying to see as many kids as possible, the things they're going through, the fights they're having, and the optimism they have, that's so moving to me."

Rivera: "The veterans hospital [in Tomah]—that was very, very moving. To see some old veterans from the Korean and Vietnam Wars. There was even one there from World War II. These guys that committed and gave so much for our country are the true heroes in America. We wanted to relay that message. [A man] had his beret on from the Vietnam War. I guess he wore this thing for a lot of years because it looked well-used. Before I left he wanted a picture, and I gave him the picture and he took off his beret and put it on my head. In return all he wanted me to do was write him a letter, so that's what I'm going to do when I get home. I'm very grateful for his gesture; it was very moving. Right now, I gotta say that's probably the best part of the trip so far. To touch somebody, a total stranger, that much, to basically give me a possession that he's had for a long time, it meant so much to him."

Nelson: "My favorite part so far has been the children's hospital. My son had a scope a couple of months ago to figure out what was wrong with him and some of his eating, so having him go through that, that was minor compared to what some of these kids are going through, but still, having such a young child put to sleep and some sort of surgery and it being out of your hands. We dealt with that a little bit. The parents are also going through a lot. A lot of people forget about the parents. There's the financial stress, the jobs, and possibly a feeling that it might be their fault. It's great to give both support."

McCarren: "I think it's been a lot of fun. There are a lot of good things going on as far as raising money and visiting different groups. Standing out for all of us is the veterans; it's so cool to be around those guys. I've [also] been impressed with the messages you [Henderson] and Charlie and others have delivered. I think it's a rip-roaring success, despite my presence." The last line he delivered in his self-deprecating Larry way.

What a shock for these kids. They certainly did not expect Packers William Henderson and Charlie Peprah to be serving up the mashed potatoes.
COURTESY OF INDIAN HILL SCHOOL

After Henderson's tour, one of the Packers people flipped channels on the television at the front, while the video and PR staffers sat at a card table in the back uploading items to the team's website. Nelson was looking at his iPad while Rivera read *Catch Me If You Can*.

"It's a good book," he said, flipping to the cover for us to see. "It's about one of the greatest con artists in history. He changed the banking industry and the way we process checks and do business in our banking system."

Others relaxed back in their seats and chatted. Soon enough we pulled up at Indian Hill elementary school in River Hills. After being with the older folks the day before at the retirement home, it was a treat to see the other side of the coin: kids in the youngest grades squealing with surprise and joy when they saw the Packers. Not only that, but the plan was for the Packers to put on latex gloves and serve them lunch from the cafeteria line.

"I got the fruit . . . ," Peprah said as he stood behind a tray of sliced cantaloupe. "My man Mason's got the rolls. My man Will Henderson, he's got the mashed potatoes. Mark Murphy is on the beef and the salad."

The teachers were just as floored—probably more so—than the kids.

Mason Crosby using his strong right leg in a different way.
COURTESY OF INDIAN HILL SCHOOL

"It was a total surprise. We knew we had a guest coming, but we didn't know who the guests actually were," a kindergarten teacher told me.

"And your reaction?" I asked.

"Blown away!" she said, her eyes still registering shock.

To see these gridiron heroes dishing potatoes onto the kids' trays was heartwarming. The players sat at the long cafeteria tables and chatted with the pint-size crowd, many of whom were one-third their size. Big guys like Rivera had to squish their bodies into the tiny seats.

Then came recess.

The back doors to the cafeteria led out to a blacktop, a grassy area, and a climbing structure. All of the folks—kids and Packers alike—went bursting through those doors into a warm, spring sunshine with huge smiles across their faces.

We hardly knew where to start shooting video first. Over here you had Nelson, Super Bowl hero, pushing kids on the swings. Turn right and you saw one of the top kickers in the league, Crosby, as well as former team safety Peprah right in the middle of a soccer game.

You can almost hear the squeals and laughter in this picture as Marco Rivera adds a couple of kids to his weight-training routine. COURTESY OF INDIAN HILL SCHOOL

Look that way and Super Bowl champ Rivera had kids attached to each bicep as he lifted them off the ground.

Another Super Bowl champion, Henderson, was going down the tube slide with the kids, his chiseled body emerging from the bottom like the Pied Piper with at least a dozen small people behind him. Then Nelson found the jump rope area and dove right in. The principal and another girl were turning the rope.

"Should we go faster?" the principal asked the kids who were watching with glee.

"YES!"

Now the rope whipped around and Nelson's feet were flying off the ground. Parents nearby were shaking their heads in disbelief.

"I just came over to drop off my son's hat and the Packers are here?" a mom said to me. "I have to text my husband. He'll just die." I took a picture of her with Packers in the background.

A girl probably in second grade asked Peprah if she was dreaming.

"I'm going to pinch you," he answered with a laugh and a light tweak of her arm. "Are you dreaming?"

"I'm not dreaming," she confirmed as her two pigtails bobbed next to him.

"[Another kid] asked me, she was like, 'Did you really come all the way from Green Bay just to see me?'" Peprah told us as he surveyed the scene. "And I was like, 'Yeah, sure we did. We came just to see you.' They're pretty excited, man. This is pretty cool."

The Packers didn't just do a cursory ten minutes with these kids. They were jumping and swinging, kicking balls, and playing tag for forty-five minutes. And they took endless pictures. When the bell rang, the kids reluctantly went back to class while the Packers waved and headed to the bus. Crosby summed it up nicely, saying, "It's really special what we've been able to do to get out in the community. We're so lucky to have such a great fan base, and this is definitely the best opportunity I've had to kind of reach out and go to where they are."

Jordy Nelson can jump rope, let me tell you! The kids loved it.
COURTESY OF INDIAN HILL SCHOOL

· The principal and his wife came to the bus to take a few last pictures, and the Packers were off to their next two stops: an assisted living facility in Cedarburg followed by Grafton High School, where a huge party awaited. The next day the traveling Packers would wrap things up by helping to build a Habitat for Humanity house in Sheboygan and attending one final, giant pep rally. Our part was done, though. We waved at the bus as it drove away. Photographer Brian and I sat down in front of the school to wait for the sports producer to pick us up. Otherwise, we were stranded at Indian Hill School.

"That was pretty awesome," we all said. I called our executive producer to tell her we had such great stuff we should get it on our 4:00 show as well as the 5:00, 6:00, and 10:00. She agreed on the spot.

It was a rare chance to see the Packers interact one-on-one with fans. Too often the two are separated. They are on the field and we are in the stands. They are on television and we are in our living rooms. But on this stretch of spring in Wisconsin they were real people, having real conversations with the masses. And the biggest thing was they were enjoying it. You could see how it was grounding them, bringing them back to their actual fan base and to the importance of what they do to entertain and excite people.

THE TEAM PHOTOGRAPHERS

AND OTHER STANDOUT PACKERS PERSONALITIES

ONE OF MY FAVORITE Packers stories has to do with three guys you may never have heard of: brothers Jim and John Biever and their father, Vern.

Vern became the Packers team photographer in the 1940s; his sons followed in his footsteps, picking up his love of the lens. Jim took over for his dad as the Packers photographer; John works for *Sports Illustrated*. Vern passed away in 2010, but before that I had the pleasure of being invited to his house to do a story on the three of them for a special we were producing on the anniversary of Lambeau Field. Vern lived in a ranch-style place in Port Washington, with a beautiful backyard adjacent to a wooded area.

"I love to watch the deer," he told me as he shuffled through the house, giving us a tour. He was eighty-seven years old at the time. A bird feeder hung outside and a cardinal was eating. We admired the view for a few more minutes before settling in at his dining room table. I had asked Jim, John, and Vern to each select two of their all-time favorite Packers photographs to show us. This was not an easy task for them. Typically they would shoot between 1,000 and 1,200 pictures—*for just one game*. But each was ready with his favorites. We started with Vern. He held up a black-and-white photo and offered this description:

The wonderful Biever family before a game against New Orleans on September 17, 2006, from left: John, Vern, and Jim. COURTESY OF JIM BIEVER

"Lombardi and [former NFL commissioner Pete] Rozelle, where Lombardi was presented the first Super Bowl, at that time World Championship game, trophy. It's not an action picture, but the history involved here—we can never take that picture again. I'm very high on that picture as my number one."

Vern reached across his table for another black-and-white shot, this one showing a play on the field, his second favorite.

"I think I may have to go with the sweep taken in 1961 up in Minneapolis. Starr handing off to Jim Taylor, with Thurston and Kramer out in front. What makes the picture: Lombardi across the way. So I got all of the big wheels in there at one time."

"Sometimes you get lucky," said Jim.

"Better to be lucky than good," Vern volleyed, then turned his attention back to Lombardi.

"You know, when Lombardi moved into town things developed and the interest [in the Packers] really got high and it set us apart from the ordinary teams ... like the Bears," he said with a laugh, then added, "No, they're a good team, too."

John is the oldest son and had the great fortune to come of age during the Lombardi glory years.

"Naturally, the camera equipment was around the house and I picked it up and took an interest in it," he told us. "I got to go to Packers games."

"He was the most popular guy in high school," Vern jumped in.

In fact, John was at the Ice Bowl as a sixteen-year-old. He was helping his dad and was stationed near the end zone.

"The Packers were driving and we needed to be in two places," said John. "We needed to be on the sideline recording how Vince Lombardi was going to react, and we needed to be at the goal line to see if a touchdown was scored. It was decided I would do that portion of it."

"I gave him the easy job," Vern slipped in.

"Right," said John, chuckling. "I took the picture with a semi-pro-type camera. Bart Starr has just snuck over and Chuck Mercein is throwing his arms up showing a touchdown and Jerry Kramer is at the bottom of the pile after throwing a block. Everything worked out on that one picture."

His shot of the famous Starr sneak became one of the most well-known photos in NFL history.

Vern's favorite picture: Rozelle and Lombardi at the first Super Bowl
PHOTO BY VERN BIEVER

John is one of only four photographers to have attended every single Super Bowl. I suspected his second favorite photo might be from one of those games—but I didn't know he would be going back to his teenage years again.

"My other favorite would be after the first Super Bowl," said John, as he slid a second photo across the table. "My dad took me along to the first Super Bowl game in 1966, and this is Vince Lombardi leaving the field after the first victory, and this is my dad here on the side recording

Next pages: Vern's second favorite: Lombardi is in the trench coat in the background, watching. PHOTO BY VERN BIEVER

it from a different angle. You've got both of them in the same picture, so I'd say that's pretty high up there on the list."

"Who's the most important one there, John?" needled Vern.

"There are two legends in the photo," threw in Jim, and father and sons laughed easily. It was obvious Vern kept things light and fun around his house.

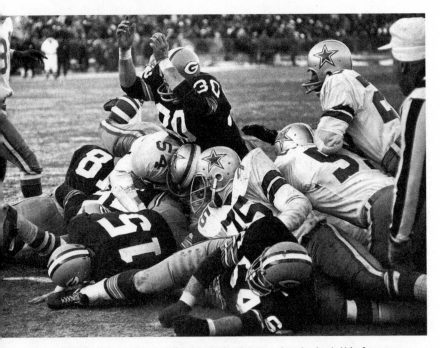

It blows me away that John was only sixteen when he took this famous picture. COURTESY OF JOHN BIEVER

Now it was time for Jim's favorites. We turned from black-and-white photos to color as both of his involved the modern era and Brett Favre. He selected one off the table showing Favre in the locker room with the rest of the team, all in full game uniform, in a circle with their heads bowed. Favre's back was to the camera, his left hand resting lightly on the shoulder of teammate Cullen Jenkins; Ryan Pickett was to his right. Two things were striking about the image: one, that Favre, the only one standing, was the dominant figure in the photo and two, that it was such a private moment inside the locker room.

John's other favorite: this was right after the first Super Bowl. He loves this photo because his dad is in it, wearing the black suit and looking off to the side. COURTESY OF JOHN BIEVER

"It's a pregame prayer. Everybody's kneeling except for Brett, and to me it drove home who the leader of that team was at the time," Jim said of the 2006 photo.

Another favorite Favre photo has him pointing to the crowd during the NFC championship game loss in 2008.

"[It's] a celebration after the last touchdown of the championship game that the Packers scored in Green Bay. A similar picture has probably been shot hundreds of times, but this has meaning that this was the last [scoring pass of Favre's Packers career] in Green Bay," noted Jim.

"It's been an experience that you'll never forget," Vern reflected, gazing down at the pictures strewn in front of him. "Having been there from almost the very beginning—1941—it's been something to see the whole [NFL] scheme develop from players playing on both sides of the ball; now it's one-sided and they're all specialists."

"It's been unbelievable as kind of a family operation," John said.

"Just being able to basically record history here has been a lot of fun," added Jim.

"Do you realize how many people would love to trade jobs with you?" I asked.

"Not available!" Vern quipped and all three laughed. Vern shot pictures from the press box until he was eighty-six.

After the interview Vern took us into his basement. The place could have been a Packers museum. Pictures were everywhere, press passes tacked to a peg board as well as a ticket stub and field photo pass to Super Bowl I. There was a darkroom with rolls of film hanging from the walls, and old programs, pennants, and mementos lined metal shelves in a room that resembled a vault. Vern was modest about this Packers treasure chest. He asked us not to shoot any of it because he didn't want to brag and also, as an older man, didn't want people to know what he had in his basement. After his death, his sons had an estate sale for many of the items. His darkroom was transported from his basement to the Packers Hall of Fame facility at Lambeau Field, and a temporary display on Vern Biever opened in September 2012, including the darkroom.

One of Jim's favorites: this was, essentially, Favre's farewell to the Packers. COURTESY OF JIM BIEVER

I found the pictures and the stories from the Bievers to be especially poignant: two generations of photographers documenting Packers history from Lombardi to Rodgers. What they had witnessed was astounding. Yet, they were so down-to-earth they still ran a travel agency out of

Port Washington in addition to their Packers duties. They were the kind of people you wished you had in your own family. Their small-town genuineness meshed perfectly with Green Bay's.

Bob Harlan, the Packers president and CEO from 1989 to 2006, was another personality whose demeanor reflected the entire idea of the Packers. He took pride in answering his own phone, even if it was a fan calling with a complaint. In 2004, Harlan was going to be inducted into the Packers Hall of Fame, and I was asked to emcee the banquet at Lambeau. I didn't want to introduce him with the standard fare that you could find in any biography, so I made arrangements through PR to spend fifteen minutes on the phone with his wife. The funny part for me was that this interview took place in the parking lot of Mayfair Mall in Milwaukee. I had just dropped one of my sons off at a class at the zoo and was on my way to buy something to wear to the event when our appointed time arrived. I scrambled to find paper and pen in the car and then proceeded to have the most pleasant conversation with Madeline Harlan one could ever imagine. I asked her what books her husband was reading, where he liked to go on vacation, what movies or TV shows he enjoyed, and how they met. The part that really stands out for me is that, at one point in talking about her husband, Madeline started to choke up. She just loved him so much she was overwhelmed talking about all of his good qualities. Later in the conversation I joked, "Does Bob have any faults? Does he leave dirty dishes in the sink or anything?" She laughed and said, "It's not easy being married to Mr. Perfect."

The week before the event we were on our annual family vacation to Minneapolis to see Paul's family. My "vacation" time there included juggling looking up background information on Harlan and the other people I'd be introducing while trying to get one-year-old Charlie to take his naps—and to keep my overtired eyes from closing themselves.

The evening itself was a wonderful tribute to Harlan and, given my deep respect for him, I wanted to give it my all as emcee. I used the majority of the tidbits Madeline had given me, including the Mr. Perfect part, at various intervals throughout the program. A few years later we produced a special on Harlan that I wrote and hosted. We started the special with me on the Robert E. Harlan Plaza right outside of the

Lambeau Field Atrium. For this half-hour segment we interviewed Bob and Madeline together, and Kevin Harlan agreed to drive to a Kansas City television station to be interviewed via satellite about his dad. I was proud of my association with the Harlans and was truly moved to be able to tell their story.

Harlan had hired Ron Wolf as general manager when the Packers were deep in their down years. Wolf was a character I enjoyed. For a guy who was in charge of a Super Bowl team, he was surprisingly approachable and often funny. My favorite line of his was "The tariff is too high," which was his way of talking about why he didn't acquire a certain player. I ran into him once at a restaurant in Green Bay. Jake was with me in a BabyBjörn. Wolf admired Jake for a moment and then crouched a bit to look him in the eye.

"Hello, Jake the Snake," he said with a smile.

Of all the times I interviewed Wolf, the one that jumps to mind took place after he had retired. I knew he had moved back to Green Bay, which surprised me because he had found a house in Maryland after retirement. I asked for a sit-down with Wolf, and the Packers obliged. We went to the interview room they have near the locker room. After shaking hands, the first thing I wanted to know was why he and his wife, Edie, were back in Green Bay.

"We thought it would be an opportunity for us to kind of relax," he said. "We like the people here; we like the area here. We like everything about this part of the country."

He told me he really wasn't doing anything with football but was "hanging around" Lambeau Field some.

"Ted Thompson allows me to come in and watch the tapes of the game. It keeps me up to date on how the Packers are playing and what they're doing. I'm a fan now, a big-time Packer fan, no question about that. And that allows me to understand what the Packers are doing. I never give advice, and [Thompson] has never asked, but if he should ask, I would certainly give it. He's done such a marvelous job here. Certainly with his draft choices, with the players that they have now, and the Packers look like they're in good shape."

Ron's son, Eliot, became the director of pro personnel for the Packers. Back then he was assistant in the personnel department. The younger

Wolf had started his scouting career at the tender age of ten by joining his dad to watch game film. I asked Wolf if being near his son was a draw that influenced his decision to return.

"Not really. It might have been for his mom," he said, laughing. "We need to stay out of his way, and we both try to do that."

The conversation turned to Favre. In 1992, Wolf had traded the Packers' first-round draft pick to the Atlanta Falcons for the unknown University of Southern Mississippi product who was regarded as talented but wild in both character and performance on the field. Wolf took a chance and it turned out to be one of the best trades in NFL history. I liked that Wolf could look at it objectively, although at the time of the interview Favre was playing for the Vikings.

"It is very neat. And, I think it probably is the best trade ever made, because look what he is: first-ballot Hall-of-Famer. He's done everything you need to do," he noted. "His career was only supposed to last four years because of a medical condition [a car accident in college required thirty inches of his intestine to be removed]. He's been in the league for over twenty seasons. He's piled up records that I don't even know what he's piled up. He's an exceptional player."

But is it hard to see Favre in a Vikings uniform, I pressed. Did he ever think that would happen?

"No, I never thought that would happen, but that's the nature of the game today. The game is a different game than what I grew up in, and it's hard for me to see him play for the Vikings. I used to like purple, and I don't care for purple now."

I also wanted to ask about Reggie White, another of Wolf's legendary acquisitions. His death at age forty-three had floored NFL fans everywhere. I knew Wolf was very pragmatic and not much for nostalgia, but White had clearly touched him in ways not many other players had. His answer:

"Surprisingly, I do think of Reggie. In some situations, I think about how he would do that, or how he would play this. I do think of him, which is rare for me, because I usually don't try to go back. I try to put everything out of my mind and go forward. I think he was such a dynamic player and person. What a tremendous presence on the field. Those were my exposures to him. Great sense of humor. He was a wonderful human being. And it's a shame that he's not here right now sharing the success of the Packers with all of us."

My final question for Wolf turned the subject back to him. Did he miss football? I thought he might say yes, that maybe that yearning was one of the reasons he moved back to Wisconsin, but he told me that 10 days a year he misses it; the other 355 not one bit. Wolf then shared how he was taking European vacations and enjoying meeting people from other cultures. For a man who was once the center of the football universe, he was impressively at ease with his new retired life.

The NFL is filled with personalities and many of them are transient. Your average assistant coach might move as many as ten times in his career. But Ron Wolf, Bob Harlan, and the Biever family all had staying power in Green Bay. Each made a monumental mark on team history and all stayed in, or returned to, Wisconsin. The Packers have a saying about "Packer People." This means employees or players who are decent and good and loyal and green and gold to their very core. These men all were Packer People and that's why they stood out from the crowd and made lasting impressions on me.

OTHER WISCONSIN SPORTS

The Badgers

Although fans often asked me, "Aren't you that Packers girl?" I did, in fact, cover other sports. Let's start with the Badgers.

Growing up in Madison I felt as though I attended the University of Wisconsin, although the most I did was take a juggling minicourse taught by a guy who had legally changed his name to Melonhead. But I followed the Badgers for years both personally and professionally. We typically covered three to four home games per year and were always sent to any bowl game they played.

I got to know and like then Badgers head coach Barry Alvarez back in the early days of my career. He seemed just fine with a woman asking him questions and answered my queries as he would have with any other reporter. I also enjoyed his wife, Cindy, with whom I spoke at length at one of the Badger Bash tailgate-type events. This was at a time when everyone was wondering if Alvarez would leave Wisconsin for greener pastures and take a job coaching at the University of Miami, for instance. We talked while the band played at one end of the room and brats were being cooked at the other. The quote from Cindy that always stuck with me was, "What if he wants to be the Joe Paterno of Wisconsin? What's wrong with that? Why is everyone thinking he wants to leave?"

Of course, this was before Paterno's terrible troubles at Penn State, but what she was referring to was the longevity. So it didn't surprise me when Alvarez stayed on as coach and eventually became the school's athletic director.

Alvarez handpicked defensive coordinator Bret Bielema to be his successor. I first met Bielema at an awards banquet where I was the emcee and he was the speaker. Sitting next to him at the head table, we started to chat and I found his story to be fascinating: here was a guy from a tiny town in Illinois who felt such loyalty to his college, the University of Iowa, that he had a tattoo of the team logo on his ankle. He was also the youngest head coach in Division I football at the time. And there was something else: his sister had tragically died in a horseback riding accident, an event that had shaped his life. Finding out all of this over salad and chicken, I knew it would be good for viewers to see an in-depth story on him.

We actually wound up doing two stories that showed his human side. We arranged these through the UW sports information staff and picked a warm summer day in 2006, his first year as head coach, to go down to his hometown for the initial interview. Bielema would take us on a tour of Prophetstown, Illinois, population just over 2,000, where he had grown up on his parents' hog farm.

When we got past the corn and into town, we found out that a print reporter had had the same idea, but that was OK; there was enough space for both of us. We would double up on traveling to Bielema's high school but interview his parents separately. Prophetstown had one Subway sandwich shop and a small main street and that was about it.

When we arrived at his parents' home just outside town, a Badgers flag hung from their garage in the heart of Illini country. We did a sit-down interview, his father telling us that his son was a hard worker but not a natural athlete. "Like they say, nobody can measure the size of a kid's heart, and he had a big heart," he told us.

We then followed Bielema in his big SUV to his old high school, where his former coach met us and walked us through the halls. On the wall was the athletic Wall of Fame and there was a picture of a young

Bielema, smiling. We interviewed him out on his high school football field. He talked about his sister, Betsy, and how she still motivated him.

He said he kept a poem she had written about the importance of friends and family close to him always.

Our day was nearly over, but I still wanted to ask him about that Iowa tattoo on his ankle.

"I've had a lot of offers to have it removed, but to me it's a symbol of who you are and where you are," he said. "I don't ever want to lose track of that."

Walking with Bret Bielema in his quaint Illinois hometown. TODAY'S TMJ4, MILWAUKEE

I thought it was a beautiful story showing the rise of a young football player to stardom as a collegiate coach. I was very happy with how the interviews turned out, but I wanted more than just his upbringing. Not long afterward, we had the idea to do "A Day in the Life of Bret Bielema," like we had with McCarthy.

Once again I talked to sports information.

"You want to follow him for a whole day?"

"Yes—from the moment he walks in the door until he goes home that night. We won't shoot anything you don't want us to, but we'd like to show people how hard these coaches work."

After Bielema gave his thumbs-up, we picked a day. Photographer Jim and I headed to Madison early in the summer of 2007, and although Bielema was not in full coaching mode yet because practices had not started, he still had a monster day. We sat in the outer football office waiting for him to arrive. I have always thought that the next best thing to getting access to someone's house is getting access to his or her office. You can tell a lot about people by the things they hold dear to them in their work space.

He strolled in a little late, checking his BlackBerry, but he was friendly and ready to go. First up: that office. His was large, with enormous windows overlooking Camp Randall. Much like McCarthy's, it had a big wooden desk at one end and a seating area at the other. The first thing Bielema did was to put reggae music on the stereo.

"The thing I know about reggae is they're usually on an island, usually wearing sandals, and usually very relaxed, which are three key components to having a good time," he told us.

He leaves reggae on all day. His feet were in flip-flops. He was wearing shorts and a Badgers pullover. He hummed along as he looked over some papers. Then he walked us around his office, pointing out things that mattered to him, including a school-made project of a penguin.

"That's from my niece."

And a pair of Badgers red and white wooden clogs.

"I'm Dutch, so someone made that for me."

He had a small figurine of Napoleon Dynamite on a shelf.

"I'm a big fan. He has sixteen different sayings." He pushed a button and Napoleon spurted a statement. "I push that every morning."

On Bielema's desk was a jar of candy.

"[Players] get nervous to come in and see the head coach, but they'll stop by for a gumball all the time," he noted.

He strolled down the hall to get coffee, smiling and yelling "Good morning!" to all of the employees.

"This is the real secret to 12–1 [their record the previous season, his first]: caffeine," he said as he poured himself a fresh cup.

Bielema's true first order of business for the day was to greet a potential recruit who was in town. We couldn't shoot this, so we had to get video of his closed door just to say he had a private meeting with a player.

Then we were off to the field, where a high school summer camp was going on. Bielema moved easily among the players and coaches, talking and laughing. Everyone sat up a little taller when he came into their space. He went to one player who was injured.

"We could amputate. Do you want us to amputate?"

The player laughed.

A couple of big boosters were waiting, and Bielema headed off to give them a private tour of the facilities, including a stop at Alvarez's office. These were the high rollers who donated a lot of money to the program and got some special access as a perk.

"OK, next thing: I have to run home and change," Bielema told us.

We went with him to the parking lot, where he had a small orange convertible sports car waiting. He hopped in and turned on the radio, put on some shiny shades, and adjusted his sun visor. Jim sat in the passenger seat, shooting Bielema driving the car, while I steered our station vehicle behind them. Bielema would wave at the occasional person and bop his head to the music the whole time. He looked sleek and in command, almost like the king of Madison.

At his house we got shots of Bielema going into the front door in his shorts and flip-flops and then coming out in the dressier clothes he needed for a banquet that night. (He understandably didn't want anyone knowing where he lived, but he gave us permission to shoot the front door.) He allowed us to sit in his living room while he changed, but anything inside was not for camera purposes. Still, we got to see the interior of his place and it was impressive—the ultimate bachelor pad (although he's since gotten married). He showed us his surround-sound stereo system ("Check out how loud this can go," he said as he cranked it up) and his well-stocked game room in the basement. We were there about ten minutes and he was changed and ready to go.

"Now I have some errands to run this afternoon and you're not allowed to follow me on those," he said. "Meet me at the banquet later."

So Jim and I went off to have lunch on our own in Madison, then found our way to the hotel where a bunch of Wisconsin boosters were meeting.

Bielema strolled in in his nice button-down shirt and immediately started schmoozing. He was the perfect football coach that way. He looked you in the eye and gave you a big handshake and was always smiling. The boosters gravitated to him. We shot for a half hour or so, running into other Badgers coaches, like Bo Ryan of the basketball team. We also saw the radio announcers, Mike Lucas and Matt Lepay.

"Hey, what are you doing here?" Lepay asked me.

"We're following Bielema for a day."

"A whole day?"

"Yup. We've been on his tail since 8:30 a.m."

"Wow, I bet that was interesting." And it was. Bret Bielema, football coach, was also Bret Bielema, regular guy from Prophetstown, Illinois, and Bret Bielema, captain confidence who radiated a good-time vibe wherever he went. We bid our good-byes to Bielema and drove back to Milwaukee. My favorite part of the story was him sitting behind his desk jamming to Bob Marley.

I covered many, many Badgers football games, but Nebraska's first foray into the Big Ten stood out. It was a crazy weekend: the Brewers were also in the playoffs, the Packers were playing, and Wisconsin sports fans' excitement was through the roof.

Paul and I drove over to Madison early with the kids. Then I had my stepdad take me downtown and drop me as close to the stadium as he could—which was still a good fifteen blocks away. The streets were so jammed with cars, we had been inching along, and walking was a lot faster. It was supposed to be a chilly day, but in the sun it was actually bordering on hot. I trekked the long hike to Camp Randall, passing bar after bar teeming with Badgers fans, music spilling out from each. I was supposed to meet my photographer in a gated area just outside the stadium for a live shot. I finally found the media entrance and was told that the area where he was stationed was clear across the field. There was only one problem: they wouldn't let me anywhere near the field while ABC set up its cameras. Don't ask me why I couldn't see the cameras being set up, but that was the rule. So I had to take catwalks and back ramps in a zigzag pattern until I finally found our people with just a few minutes to spare.

Our photographer was set up with nothing but a wall and a tiny sliver of the stadium behind him. At WTMJ we have had it drilled into our heads to show people and movement, so I told him we'd have to move to the walkway where Badgers fans were streaming past. We did three live shots there, trying to show the steady flow of fans as well as some cheerleaders nearby. In between live shots I sat on a cement curb and wrote out what I would say in the next shot. But then our anchor, Rod Burks, called.

"Dude—you gotta be careful out there. Some guy just gave the finger in the background of your shot," he told me.

Fantastic. Here we move away from the wall background to try and show life and this is what we get. From that point forward I tried to keep an eye on who might be behind me, but it is kind of hard when you're talking and gesturing and have your back turned to the crowd half the time anyway.

By the time we finished our live shots, we were half an hour from kickoff and I had to get to the press box, which I knew would be no easy task. I'm not sure if there's a worse system in America than what Camp Randall has for media. There is one small elevator that has to take suite holders, assistant coaches (they always get first priority), and the media up. There are no stairs. We all waited in the concourse, and by the time I got to my seat the band was playing the national anthem.

As for the game, the Badgers stunned all of us by absolutely steamrolling the Cornhuskers. We thought they might win, but this was total domination. The final score was 48–17. Somewhere about the third quarter, Rod called, saying, "I need you to do a 10:00 live shot for me."

"But the game won't be over," I responded.

"I know, but it looks good to have presence."

"OK, but you realize anyone who cares is watching the game, right?"

"Yes, but we still need a 10:00 live shot."

So, I hauled myself back down the elevator, through the stands, and out to the parking lot where we did a live shot showing the police mounted on horses behind us—ready in case a riot broke out among exuberant Badgers fans (it didn't). The clock wound down and the game ended just as we wrapped up. My photographer and I then hustled to the interview area. The Badgers always bring Bielema to a press conference area and have players available for questions in the weight room. Unlike the NFL, college ball that I've covered gives no locker room access.

The press conference was packed; I had to scrunch down in front of our camera. Reporters are constantly trying to shout questions over each other and you have to be quick and assertive if you want to get a query in. The room buzzes with "Bret . . . Bret . . ." after every answer as reporters vie to get Bielema's head to turn their way. I asked Bielema about Nick Toon's day—he had had an amazing catch—and then my photographer and I went to the weight room to interview quarterback Russell Wilson and the other guys. When they bring a player out they yell his name—"Russell Wilson!"—and set him up in a spot. At any given time there could be ten players doing interviews with little pods of people around them. Wilson had the biggest crowd that day. Finally, at about 11:15 p.m. we went to shoot standups in the empty stadium.

By the time our photographer dropped me back at my parents' house, it was nearly midnight. I snuck in to see my mom and stepdad just turning off the TV; everyone else was already in slumberland. I got a snack and flipped channels for a while, then went to hit the pillow, knowing the kiddos would be up bright and early and ready to play. This was often the most grueling part about working in sports. It was nearly always a night shift and it's difficult to come down right after doing your job for nine hours, especially if you've been at a noisy and exciting football game with adrenaline going. Yet, you start to feel panicky knowing your children will want your attention the second they get up. After all, they've been waiting to see you and need mommy time. You want to be at your best for them, but you're just plain tired. This work was much easier to manage before I had kids. I crawled into bed and prayed for sleep to come, knowing, too, that a few days later I'd be on to the Brewers as they continued their postseason run.

Bielema continued in his position for six more years—until the day he blindsided everyone by taking a job at the University of Arkansas. The shocking part was not that he left, but that it came just three days after the Badgers had clinched a third consecutive Rose Bowl berth. Even Alvarez had no clue; he later told the story that Bielema called him from his New York City hotel room saying he needed to talk. The two were in Manhattan for the National Football Foundation awards dinner. Bielema arrived in Alvarez's room and told him his plans. Alvarez recounted part of this exchange days later at a press conference in Madison. "I said, 'You're not telling me you're going to visit with the Arkansas people. You've already taken the job?'"

The answer was yes, there would be no chance for a counter offer. Bielema had his mind made up to go to the SEC, college football's most powerful conference.

I was in the sports office the following day, December 5, 2012, the day the story broke nationally. My schedule that morning was to shoot and write a feature story on a deaf speedskater who was gunning for the 2014 Olympic Games. This was an inspiring piece and I had just handed the script and video off to our photographer, Jeff Janca, to edit when I heard the voice of our executive sports producer Rick Rietbrock. "Uh-oh—did you guys see this Yahoo report?"

Larry McCarren was in the office as well. He had recently joined WTMJ after leaving his Green Bay station. Larry and I went on with the lead story on the 3:00 and 4:00 newscasts. In between, I had to switch to mom mode and run to Charlie's school to pick him up, then deliver him home for a snack, discuss his homework, and get him settled. After Paul came dashing back from a shoot to take over on the home front, I was back to the station, making calls, trying to get phone interviews with former Badgers and other people with knowledge or insight into the situation, like Lepay, the radio voice of the Badgers. We all bantered back and forth about whether Alvarez himself might coach. I didn't think he would, but I was wrong.

Several players had asked Alvarez to consider stepping back from his athletic director role to guide the team at the Rose Bowl and he agreed. What a turn of events for the players, the assistant coaches, Alvarez himself, and all of the Badger fans who were suddenly not so happy with Bielema.

Alvarez had won every Rose Bowl he had been a part of, a perfect 3–0. Bielema had lost his two. But on January 1, 2013, the Alvarez streak came to an end with a 20–14 loss to Stanford. After the game, Bielema tweeted his congratulations on a great year.

The Brewers

The Milwaukee Brewers were the first team I was truly a fan of, so it felt like coming full circle to cover them. From my youth, I remember sitting in the stands at County Stadium on an end-of-year field trip in seventh grade. It was freezing and the wind was whipping. Then it started to rain. This was way before the roof was built, and on bad weather days (almost all spring) there would be next to no one in the stands except for those unlucky enough to be on a seventh-grade field trip.

With the team playing eighty-one home games per year, WTMJ didn't go to every single one, but we were out at Miller Park often enough to get to know the team well. It was a treat to cover a team that was just fifteen minutes from our station, not two hours like the Packers. I don't think there's another market in the country where the largest city is so far from its main football team.

I covered opening day seventeen straight times, many of them on the daybreak shift, which meant getting up at 3:00 a.m. and being on the air (and supposedly looking somewhat fresh) at 5:00 a.m. I'm not an early morning person and that alarm clock blaring while it's still dark doesn't match my body's circadian rhythm. I may be the only person drinking a Diet Coke at 4:30 a.m., I'd think. I would tell myself that at least I got to see a pretty sunrise, and our group breakfast at IHOP every year after the show ended at 7:00 a.m. was a fun reward. But opening day often fell during spring break, and my family usually had somewhere we were trying to get to, so I hated this assignment for personal reasons. One year I left the stadium and went right to the airport to fly to DC for a family vacation; another time to catch a flight to New York.

I did try to make the most out of it by pitching the idea that we do a "Miller Park Is Waking Up" story with a timeline. This made it a lot more fun because we could show the first workers arriving and polishing each seat and the sound system being tested. Our photographer Brian added the time of day—"5:20 a.m.," "6:45 a.m.," and so on—to the video and we were happy with it. The strange part was that when everyone else started rolling into the stadium at 10:00 a.m., my day was practically over. Stranger still was being there all morning and going home or on a family vacation before the actual game started. I had to read the score on my phone from our hotel room on the East Coast.

I always had a tremendous amount of respect for Bud Selig. Here was a car salesman who became the commissioner of Major League Baseball. A former owner of the Brewers, he maintains an office in a building overlooking Lake Michigan and has never become a big shot. He or his secretary would always return calls, and he was always thoughtful and kind in his demeanor.

His daughter Wendy Selig-Prieb ran the Brewers for a while, and I did a personal sit-down with her early in my career. I remember her saying that her daughter's first word was *Brewers*, and I remember that I was a little too sappy, over-the-top in the story about how great she was. So much so that a viewer called to complain.

"How should I have done it differently?" I asked Dennis Krause, the sports director.

"You could have asked her about the perception that she was handed the job because of her family name," was his response. Another lesson learned.

A few years later I wanted to do a series on "Famous Siblings" and I asked Selig-Prieb if we could interview her sister, Sari, who was a "regular person": a stay-at-home mom in a Milwaukee suburb. Wendy called her and she agreed to an interview.

We went to Sari's very attractive house and talked with her and her kids. It was an interesting piece because she had the same upbringing as Wendy but followed a completely different route. She said she just wasn't ever that into baseball, certainly not enough to want to run the team. She was content and happy. Not having a sibling myself I envied the closeness of Sari and Wendy and the fact that each was completely comfortable in her own skin. I also wished I had had a father to rival theirs—not because he's famous or rich or in baseball circles, but because he allowed them to be who they were and supported each of them.

As an only child, I was always curious about the dynamic of having a brother or sister, which is what fascinated me about doing "Famous Siblings." I also interviewed the sibling of Packers wide receiver Bill Schroeder, but unfortunately the idea died after that. I got busy with other things and never found enough other subjects.

I really came to like most of the Brewers players and coaches. Baseball players on the whole seem to be the most relaxed bunch of professional athletes there are, probably because they play nearly every day so there's not a week of buildup to each game like there is in football, not as much hype and pressure, and certainly not as many devastating injuries. They get used to having reporters around all the time and most of them appear to have a good deal of fun in the clubhouse (the baseball word for locker room). The best was when they put on their "sweep suits"—their fun way of describing why they dressed up in their nicest clothing for the flight home—after taking a series, or when they made the rookies wear ridiculous Halloween costumes—everything from a piece of pizza to a French maid—on the team plane.

I was in the clubhouse when the Brewers clinched a playoff spot in 2008, their first since 1982. The players were all sitting in the dining room part of the clubhouse watching the Mets game on TV. If the Mets lost to the Florida Marlins, the Brewers were in. If the Mets won, the series went to a one-game playoff. You could feel the tension and hear the players' voices rising and falling as they cheered on the Marlins. Then came the final out—and a Mets loss—and chaos ensued. The players burst through the doors and into the main section of the clubhouse that was prepped with plastic everywhere to protect everything from champagne. The sight of pure joy on their faces as they ran, arms in the air, from the dining room, inspired chills.

Veterans and rookies grabbed bottles of bubbly from the tubs in the middle of the room and started spraying—and we got so wet we had to laugh. My assignment was to interview coaches and owner Mark Attanasio, so we focused our camera on interim manager Dale Sveum and Brewers great Robin Yount, who had come off the bench, so to speak, from his retirement in Arizona to help Sveum for a few weeks. In the middle of the madness, the two shared the biggest, most champagne-drenched hug I have ever seen, yelling and screaming and pounding each other on the back. "We did it! We did it!" they kept shouting. I felt my eyes water and it wasn't from Asti Spumante. It was a sight. Merriment and satisfaction that raw is a rare thing.

We found Attanasio and interviewed him while he wore swim goggles to protect his eyes.

"Attanasio in the goggles was my favorite part of the whole night. I just cracked up," one of our producers said later.

It was a great moment in Brewers history, but unfortunately the euphoria did not last long. The Brewers had to go to Philadelphia to face the mighty Phillies, and they had a major problem: other than C. C. Sabathia, they had almost no usable pitchers. Ben Sheets was hurt and Jeff Suppan was not having a good year. They wound up sending one of the most unexpected starters of all time to the mound: Yovani Gallardo, who had missed an entire year with a terrible injury sustained while tripping over first base. His first start in a year came in the playoffs. He pitched decently, but the Brewers lost that game and then lost again when Sabathia pitched on short rest. The day Sabathia started I was at Charlie's soccer game, listening to the game on headphones. So was another player's dad, and when Sabathia gave up a grand slam to Shane Victorino, the dad took off his headphones and threw them to the ground.

The Brewers won only one game in the series and were eliminated.

They got back into the playoffs in 2011. The night they clinched I was on standby at home just in case it looked like they might win and a celebration would be happening. But I had a bad cold and was lying on the couch trying to summon up enough energy to go in case I was needed. Lo and behold, the Brewers were leading in the late innings and a call came in, telling me to go down to the stadium and meet the photographer. I had to drag myself there but perked up almost immediately as the atmosphere was—to use the old cliché—electric.

This time the team was hoping to clinch a division title. They had just won and needed the Cardinals to lose to the Cubs. Players and fans alike were on the field and in the stands watching that game unfold on the Jumbotron after the Brewers game ended. With a couple of outs to go, players retreated to the clubhouse and so did we. We were allowed to stand off to the side, awaiting the eruption that would come if St. Louis lost. There was champagne in tubs and plastic covered everything once again.

Boom! The Cardinals lost and madness again ensued. It's hard to fully describe a baseball celebration. Players are jumping up and down like kangaroos and dancing and singing and laughing and screaming and spraying and spraying and spraying champagne. Someone will be talking and another player will sneak up behind him and dump a bottle of liquid over his head. I was thinking I might be able to stay somewhat on the fringes this time and not get too wet, when Nyjer Morgan, the team's jokester and oversize personality who refers to himself as "Tony Plush," his alter ego, came over snickering and making a point of spraying all available reporters. Almost immediately, my eyes started to sting. Champagne and corneas do not mix. But we soldiered on, talking to Prince Fielder, Ryan Braun, the new manager Ron Roenicke, and many other Brewers in the middle of the celebration. This time around almost everyone was wearing goggles and I wished I had thought to buy a pair—or at least bring some that my kids used at their swim classes.

As we walked around the soaked clubhouse, a champagne cork rolled right at my feet and stopped at my toes. I picked it up and tucked it into my pocket; it became a souvenir I showed the kids the next day. They thought it was pretty awesome that the Brewers had actually touched this cork.

The celebration spilled onto the field as thousands of Brewers fans moved into the first few rows of the stadium to yell and scream and

Brewers clubhouse, September 23, 2011: the energy in that room was like nothing else.
TODAY'S TMJ4, MILWAUKEE

pump their fists with the players who had returned to the field. I was now champagne-soaked, my hair feeling sticky and heavy. We saw Braun's girlfriend in the middle of the pack, and I asked her if she would do an interview with us. She was tall and thin, a model, and very young looking. Our female anchor was so excited that we had Braun's girlfriend that she insisted we use it

in a tease for the 10:00 show: "Meet Ryan Braun's girlfriend! Tonight at ten!" In my experience women *love* seeing players' wives and girlfriends.

Back on the field John Axford was going down the line of fans hugging each and every one of them. Prince Fielder, who is naturally shy, seemed to be out of character as he did the same. He posed for pictures with a group of young men who immediately turned to each other and said, "We got a picture with Prince Fielder! Text it now! That's going to be my screen saver!" Fielder was getting bear hugs from fans who were imploring him to stay in Milwaukee and not leave in free agency.

"Please, Prince, we need you here."

He would only smile and say, "We'll see, we'll see."

After he pulled himself away from the throngs and back to where his wife and two young sons were standing, I asked him how it felt to be embraced by the fans like that.

"Oh, man, it's fun," he said. "They're so excited."

"You know they all want you back, right?"

"Yeah, yeah, I know. We just have to wait and see how it all plays out."

But we all pretty much guessed Fielder was as good as gone, and, sure enough, his agent, the infamous Scott Boras, got him a monster deal in Detroit. He packed up and left Milwaukee for good that off-season.

As the night wore on the players started to get tired. Their voices were hoarse from celebrating and many began to filter back to the clubhouse and out to their cars. There was one guy, though, who sat looking blissfully content: Rickie Weeks. He was in the dugout, perched on the long bench with his girlfriend on another riser just behind him, and he was smoking a big stogie. He had the most peaceful, happy look on his face as he surveyed the field now littered with confetti and a few stray

champagne bottles. I wasn't sure if he would let us get a shot of him in this blissful state, so I tried to catch his eye as we set up the camera just to make sure it was OK. He glanced at us and gave us a Zen-like smile before flashing a peace sign. I knew he was fine with it.

Our photographer rolled about thirty seconds of video of Weeks, and it was the last shot we used in our celebration piece.

The Brewers went on to beat the Diamondbacks in a tough five-game series to advance to the National League Champion-

Rickie Weeks enjoying the moment right after he gave a little "yeah, it's cool to tape me" nod. TODAY'S TMJ4, MILWAUKEE

ship Series, but they ran completely out of gas and saw their pitching staff blow up against the Cardinals. St. Louis was on a late-season tear much like the Packers of 2010, when they plowed to the Super Bowl victory. The Brewers won the first game of the series, lost one at home, and went to St. Louis tied 1–1. But fans could already feel they were on shaky ground. The Brewers defense disappeared, their starting rotation fell apart, and the Cardinals won two of the next three. The Brewers returned home needing to win the final two games to advance to the World Series; the Cards needed just one win. I was sent to Miller Park on the Saturday before the game, an off day for the players, with just optional workouts. Unfortunately, I came out of the locker room feeling they were going to lose. There was a defeatist attitude, a complete lack of spirit and confidence. The interviews we got were flat and dry. There was no Fielder, no Braun available in the clubhouse. When your best players, your team leaders, avoid the media, you know things are on edge.

We did talk to one player who had made a bad mistake the night before—letting a ball go right past him—but he was almost baffled as to why we would ask if he felt bad or was using the error as motivation. He looked at us like we were crazy.

"I hate to say this, but I think they're goners," I told my producer. "It's the same look the Bears had in the NFC championship." It's amazing how much you can read a team just based on their demeanor. Swagger and confidence really do count for something. The Cards had it that year and won the World Series. The Brewers' big shot fizzled into the October chill.

That offseason we all wondered what the heck was going on with Ryan Braun, the National League MVP. He gave the appearance of being the epitome of a squeaky clean all-American, yet he had tested positive for performance-enhancing drugs in December and MLB issued a fifty-game suspension. Had he really taken steroids? Was it all some terrible mistake? Did he have herpes? That was the hot rumor for a while: that medication for an STD caused a spike in his testosterone. We had reporters Googling *herpes meds* trying to see if increased testosterone was a side effect. It wasn't.

The story broke in early December and some fans were furious with ESPN for reporting on it as, back then, steroid testing and results were supposed to remain private business. All the same, everyone jumped on it. We had to wait until late February, the day before spring training started, for the ruling to come down from MLB on whether his suspension would stand.

I was working the day Braun-gate really exploded. Tweets came across from an ESPN reporter saying the story would break or we would finally get the verdict "today" and "soon." Within seconds, the assistant news director was literally running into the sports office.

"I need you to be ready to jump on live anytime," he told me.

"Yup, I figured. I'm just getting some makeup on. Should we go on with what we know now and say it looks like it will definitely be today?"

"Yes, but be sure to credit ESPN in case they're wrong."

So I jumped onto the "robo-cam" set—which is where a camera is set up in the corner of the newsroom instead of the studio to show the bustle of people behind the reporter—and within a few minutes they had the "breaking news" music playing and the anchors were tossing to me for updates. The next ninety minutes were complete chaos as two reports came down simultaneously, one saying he was exonerated and one saying the suspension was upheld. We reported both at first, saying, "We're getting conflicting information . . . someone is wrong and we're working to find out who." Twelve minutes later the Associated Press issued a retraction to their story about the suspension being upheld. They called it a "typo." How on God's green earth that can happen, I do not know, and they looked terrible, but we now had confirmation from many sources as various national and local reporters got the correct information out within seconds of each other: Braun had become the first known Major League Baseball player in history to have a ruling overturned. We stayed on the air nonstop from about 4:00 or 5:30 with the story, then picked it up again at 6:00 and 10:00 and carried Braun's press conference live in its entirety the next day.

I thought Braun was very believable in talking to the media and explaining his side. He nailed it. He essentially blamed a faulty testing process and laid suspicion at the feet of the local man who collected the test, stored it in his basement fridge, and took it to FedEx to be sent to the lab days later. Braun said the tester had not followed protocol; the man later insisted he had. But I thought Braun's most powerful argument came when he told people to look at the numbers. His stats had not changed monumentally in years. Of course there was some fluctuation in his batting average and other markers, as there would be for any ballplayer, but the time it took him to run from home plate to first base, for example, was exactly the same. If he had taken steroids, he argued, how could that be? Was he guilty or innocent? We probably will never know the true answer, but he presented his case well. The following year he put up MVP-type numbers again and there was no way he could have been juicing that season—if he had ever been. After a positive result less than twelve months earlier, the amount of scrutiny and testing on him by Major League Baseball would have been too much for him to outmaneuver. What really happened with that one plastic cup? There are some mysteries in sports and in life that will never be unraveled. The story of Braun's urine sample may be one of them.

Olympians

Other than the Badgers and the Brewers, I had the great fortune to cover a number of Olympians as well.

For some reason as I was growing up my less-than-enthusiastic-about-sports family would gather every four years to watch the Olympics, particularly the Winter Games. Snuggling on the couch with my dad—on a rare day he was around—while oohing and aahing ski jumpers and figure skaters is one of the few good memories I have with him. I still recall a joke I made up and tried out for my family when I was just ten.

"I hear your son is in the Olympics. Is he a winner?"

"No, he's a luger."

This is why I did not become a comedian. But I developed a deep love for the Olympics, and meeting people who are the absolute best in the world at their sport is thrilling. It was also refreshing to cover sports that were off the beaten path.

The first truly great Olympian I had a brush with was Bonnie Blair. It was 1994 and she was fresh off the Lillehammer Olympics, where she had added two more gold medals to her already remarkable collection. WTMJ and the Pettit National Ice Center were having a welcome-home celebration and I had been asked by our station to be one of the emcees. She was going to do some emcee and speaking duties, too. Blair was about as warm and approachable as anyone could be, and the thing I remember most is that she signed my program afterward: "To Jessie, Great Job!! Bonnie Blair." It meant so much to me, I hung it up in my office where it still remains.

In 2012 we did a story with Blair, a where-are-they-now piece. I met her at her preteen daughter's gymnastics school and then interviewed Blair at her home, where she had a coffee table specially designed in the shape of Olympic rings. Trophies of all kinds lined the mantel, but family pictures outnumbered anything else. Blair was completely happy being a devoted stay-at-home mom with the occasional speaking engagement. She told of a rough few months of adjustment right after retiring—once bursting into tears as she went on a run and realized that, at that time of year, she normally would be on the speedskating circuit in Germany. But other than that, Blair had transitioned from sports and the spotlight to a normal life beautifully. As we were leaving, she was picking up a baseball glove to play catch with her high school son.

With the Pettit (one of the only ice ovals in the country) just a few minutes from downtown Milwaukee, we did tons of stories on speedskaters. One skater I kept an eye on from an early age was Casey FitzRandolph, who would win gold in 2002. But I first got to know him when he was still in school at Carroll College in Waukesha. I met him on campus and we did a story about how he tried to juggle skating and schoolwork. His license plate said "Gold 98." He didn't have the year right, but he wasn't far off. FitzRandolph was from Verona, near Madison, and over the years we did many stories with him and his parents, who were accommodating and kind. His dad, Jeff, became a starter for speedskating events because of his son's passion. He and his wife, Ruthie, invited us to a send-off party for Casey one year. Then in 2002 and 2006, two of the three times Casey represented the United States at the Olympics, WTMJ contracted with them to do something personal for us from the Games. The idea was that the station would provide them with a video camera and a FedEx account number (this was before YouTube) and they would shoot home video of their experiences in Utah and Italy and send them back to us to edit and air. I drove to their house in Verona and went over the instructions for the video camera. They lived in a glass-and-brick home, which was practically a piece of art itself, nestled in the quiet woods with only a country bar down the road from them.

The videos they sent back from both Salt Lake City and Torino were priceless. They were rolling as they got lost looking for the apartment they had rented in Italy. They gave us a tour of the apartment and showed how the hosts had left traditional Italian foods out for them. They took us around as they went to the speedskating venue and took in the street scenes at night. Ruthie; Casey's sister, Jessi; and his fiancée, Jenn, went shopping and showed viewers around the hospitality houses that were everywhere. These were places where families could hang out and relax, with free food and usually TVs tuned to whatever event was taking place. Casey brought the camera into the athletes' village for rare looks at the facilities—everything from the cafeteria to the post office.

But the best thing was the FitzRandolphs' reaction when Casey won. Jeff was shooting from the stands. As soon as he realizes Casey is the gold medalist, he whoops for joy and starts running, camera rolling, through the stands and down to the ice. His voice is breaking with emotion as he tells the security guy, "That's my son! My son just won gold!"

"Casey, Casey—way to go!" His voice is still cracking. I'm certain this absolutely human moment brought tears to more than just my eyes.

Then the FitzRandolphs took the camera to the medal ceremony in an outdoor plaza and we got to see their view as they panned the camera from them in the stands to Casey on the stage in front of millions of viewers, back to them as the family screamed and cried. This video really helped enhance our Olympic coverage. There is nothing like seeing something like that from the point of view of family members.

In 2010 we decided to keep up our station's tradition of sending a video camera with an Olympian, but by then Casey was retired. So we hooked up with a new Olympian speedskater, Jilleane Rookard, and her coach, Kip Carpenter, who had won a bronze in Salt Lake City. Rookard was training at the Pettit when I heard from a worker there that she also was the disc jockey at a local roller-skating rink. This was too good of a story to pass up, so we took the camera to Incredi-Roll and got her in the DJ booth, making the disco ball spin and playing the teeny-bop sounds. She said she was often so sore from her training workouts that she would sit in the DJ booth with ice packs on her legs.

She was also a great roller skater and a former inline skater, and she zipped around the rink helping kids who had fallen down and encouraged them all to dance. The best part was when fellow speedskater Trevor Marsicano joined her. He was her boyfriend and came to

Verona's Casey FitzRandolph, celebrating with his then girlfriend, now wife, Jenn, right after his victory at the 2002 Winter Olympics in Salt Lake City. He was the first American man to win speedskating gold in the 500 meters since another Wisconsin product, Eric Heiden, in 1980. COURTESY OF THE FITZRANDOLPH FAMILY

Incredi-Roll to see her and to blow off steam during this grueling training time. To see the two of them couple skating in the empty rink, with twinkling drops of light from the disco ball, was beyond precious. Rookard had grown up in Michigan, the child of parents who were roller-rink owners. Her story was especially moving because her mom had passed away recently and she was trying to fulfill her Olympic dream for both of them.

Rookard agreed to take a video camera for us and sent back great stuff of her and Marsicano taking the subway in Vancouver and shopping in the massive Olympic stores. She had such a bubbly personality we called it "Jill Cam," and it was a big hit in our Olympic coverage. That year Marsicano won silver in the team pursuit. Rookard did not medal but is still competing.

We also had Kip Carpenter provide footage for "Kip Cam." His video was interesting in a different way because he was extremely upset with US Speedskating for not allowing him and other private coaches full access to their athletes at the venues. He shot video showing us how far he had to sit up in the stands—behind a roped-off area, yelling down to Rookard and his other skaters. He found another private coach, Nancy

Swider-Peltz, and the two of them vented about US Speedskating as they sat outside, banned from being inside altogether at certain times of the day.

Kip Cam and Jill Cam were good investments by the station. One video camera got us a ton of exclusive, behind-the-scenes footage and allowed the personalities of the athletes and coaches to really shine.

An Olympian I always really admired was Chris Witty. Witty is a three-time medalist born in West Allis—right down the street from the Pettit. I interviewed her many times over the years, but the one thing that stands out the most is how she came forward about being sexually abused by a neighbor as a child. She had hidden it for years but wanted to open up to help other girls and women in similar situations. I asked her about it during a media day interview at the Pettit as we overlooked the oval below us. She was open and honest, and after the taping there was something I wanted to tell her. I pulled her aside, away from the camera.

"Chris, I just wanted you to know that you already made a difference in one person's life—mine. There's a guy in my neighborhood who has been bothering me for years. He'll drive by and honk or drive slowly by, looking me up and down. He once followed me to the post office. I wanted to tell you that after reading what you had to say about standing up for yourself I got up the courage to call him and ask him directly to leave me alone. I want to thank you for that. I thought to myself, 'If Chris Witty doesn't put up with it, I won't either.'"

"Wow, thanks," said Witty with empathy. "I can see where it would really bug you—it's an invasion of privacy."

"Yes, I just thought you should know you have made a positive impact."

She gave me a hug and I felt a little choked up. Women helping women means something to me, and I had a lot of pent-up emotions from feeling borderline stalked for years. Witty moved permanently to Salt Lake to train. I always wondered if she wanted a change of scenery from any bad memories she might have had in the old neighborhood. Her brother worked at a local bank for years, and Paul would bump into him every time he went to cash a check.

"Did you see Chris Witty's brother?" I always asked.

"Yup, nice guy." Nice family. Another brother, Mike, became a speedskating coach and also worked as a paramedic. After he had a child, I would occasionally run into him at summer festivals, his child on his shoulders. I have always been grateful to Chris for being the person she is.

It's amazing to me, as a parent, to think of having your child grow up to be an Olympian. Over the years I interviewed as many Olympic parents as athletes. Oftentimes they are still in Wisconsin while their kids are halfway around the world. Their houses are usually identifiable by the American or Olympic flag flying outside; the inside tends to be filled with pictures of their loved one. We interviewed Milwaukee swimmer Garrett Weber-Gale's parents before they left for the Olympics the year he won a gold medal with Michael Phelps in that amazing 400-meter freestyle relay during which their teammate's hand barely touched the wall. *Sports Illustrated* later ran an underwater picture looking up at the swimmers showing that it was literally a fingertip difference between the United States and pre-race-favorite France. The times were 3:08:24 for the United States and 3:08:32 for France. There is also the famous shot of Weber-Gale and Phelps in a moment of pure-adrenaline celebration immediately after the wall touch on the pool deck. Weber-Gale has his arm around Phelps in an embrace as both are open-mouthed with arms up in the air. It is widely considered one of those iconic moments in Olympic history. Weber-Gale swam the second leg of that race.

When I visited with Weber-Gale's mother and father, two completely down-to-earth people, they showed me baby pictures of Garrett and took me to his room, which was stocked top to bottom with shiny medals he had won over the years. They were in Beijing when their son won gold, and we communicated via e-mail. Mark Gale's note was overflowing with exclamation points and joy.

"Congratulations!! Can you tell us what the exact moment was like for you?" I wrote back. He gave us a detailed account that we used on the air that night. "We are out of our minds. As so many of you saw, judging from the churn of notes, Garrett was part of an absolutely fantastic race. People are calling it the best relay of all time. I picked up Jason Lezak's tiny little mom when it was over (Jason out-touched the

Frenchman who has been talking smack), spun her around, and told her I might just kiss her son on the lips when I see him. WOO HOO. USA. USA. USA."

WTMJ rarely sends anyone to cover the Olympics, especially if it is happening in a time zone far away. It was expensive and the hourly difference too great to make it worthwhile, so we fashioned ways to get exclusive or unusual video and comments for viewers. E-mail helped a lot, and eventually Twitter and Facebook became our best Olympic friends.

One year we went to the home of speedskater Tucker Fredricks in Janesville. He's an only child, like me, and I immediately connected with his young and relaxed parents. They also showed us a room filled with awards—a perfectly preserved museum to Tucker and his accomplishments. We did a live shot from his bedroom, interviewing his mom.

The part I liked best about their house is the growth chart on the wall next to the kitchen. With markers, crayons, pen, and the occasional knife mark they have charted the progress of Tucker from when he was a toddler to a grown man. It's very touching.

Out in the dining room they had Italian phrasebooks spread across the table since they would be taking off for the Games after the opening ceremonies but in time to see Tucker's race. Because they were going to be watching the opening ceremonies from home, we asked if we could watch with them, and, good people that they are, they said sure, come on down, and what do you like to drink because we'll pick up some beverages.

The night of opening ceremonies we parked our huge satellite truck outside their split-level home, stirring the curiosity of neighbors in their subdivision, I'm sure. Charlie was only three, so he stayed home, but I have asked if I can bring Jake along for the festivities and the Fredrickses seemed delighted to have a young face in the house again. Jake was seven. It's a bit of a late night for him but also exciting. So it's me, Paul, Jake, and Dan and Shawn Fredricks on the lookout for their son to walk across the arena with the rest of the US contingency. We watched every other nation and, finally (alphabetical order being what it is), came the United States. We're all pumped, but Jake was also getting tired and started to get a little whiny and loud.

"Jakie—look for Tucker. Jakie—this is their son, honey. It's really important to them to be able to see him and to listen to what the announcers are saying," I said.

Jake had been a perfect angel all night, sipping 7UP and eating pretzels, and now all of a sudden he's not going to ruin the moment for them, is he? Shawn smiled at us in a mom way. Luckily, Jake's tantrum was short-lived and he settled back in time to catch Tucker.

"There he is, there he is!" we all yelled. I had to do a 10:00 live shot showing video of them at the moment they saw their son, and then we took a tired Jake back to my parents' house in Madison where we're all sleeping. Tucker did not medal that year, but I will never forget watching the opening ceremonies with his two glowing parents.

Shani Davis is one of America's most famous speedskaters, not only because he's phenomenally talented, but also because he's a black man in a traditionally white man's sport. His story is a good one. He was a fast roller skater as a kid. At the time, his mother was working for an attorney whose son was an elite speedskater. The lawyer suggested Davis try speedskating, and it took off from there. His mother eventually moved from the South Side of Chicago so they could be closer to a rink in Evanston. She also woke him up early most mornings so he could get in a mile run. He always credited her for his success. He grew up to excel to the highest levels despite essentially shunning the system and coaching himself much of the time. That was just his nature.

His reputation took a hit at the 2006 Olympic Games, when he was curt to a national TV reporter. The exchange went like this:

NBC reporter Melissa Stark: "You are the first African American male to win a gold medal at the Winter Games. How proud are you of that?"

Davis: "I'm pretty happy about it."

Stark: "Just, that's it?"

Davis: "Yeah."

That didn't endear him to the public. So I was a little wary of what kind of mood we would find him in when we set up a one-on-one with him one morning at the Pettit, where he was training in between the 2006 and 2010 Olympics. He strolled in a little late but was apologetic and about as cordial as could be, although just a little reserved in an Aaron Rodgers, I'm-not-going-to-spill-my-soul-to-you kind of way. I asked him how he had changed since the last Olympics. He started by explaining why he had been a little disrespectful.

"Under the circumstances I was extremely stressed out and I acted the way I only knew how to act," he said. "I've figured things out for the best. The things that happened in 2006, even though they were negative, as a human being you have to learn to put positive spins on things that are negative and learn from those things. And I think I've learned from it."

He had also changed his tone on answering questions about being in a largely white sport. He was more than willing to talk about being a trailblazer:

"African American people aren't very interested in winter sports so much because there aren't a lot of successful African Americans doing them. Hopefully I can change that but not only for African Americans, just for everybody that's interested in doing something different. I want to be able to say this is where I came from—and where I came from people did basketball, football, track and field—but I chose to do speedskating and hopefully, if they find themselves in similar situations, they can find motivation from me."

I liked Davis. I liked that he bucked the system and the odds and accomplished his dream: he's the winner of two Olympic golds and two silvers. He also seemed to be someone who would have only a few friends but would be intensely loyal to them; I could see where he would be fun to hang out with. We talked about his training and his hobbies, and he took us down to the bowels of the Pettit where he polished the blades on his skates and did warm-up glides, moving from side to side across the carpet in front of a large mirror.

"We won't take up too much of your time. We just need a little b-roll," I told him. (B-roll is not the interview but the video of the natural actions of a human being not being prompted that you see accompanying a story.)

"Don't worry about it. I don't mind. Got any other questions?"

He seemed genuinely willing to sit and chat, and he explained in great detail the process he went through daily to keep those glistening skates in tip-top shape. We went back to the ice and got video of him zipping around. Davis was doing laps so fast we could hardly keep up as we moved the camera around. (I had once tried to move in speedskates and fell in about three seconds.) The grace and balance it takes to speedskate at any level—let alone that level—is amazing. The name Shani is Swahili for *lightweight* and that fit him perfectly—he seemed to float across the ice with a mix of speed, power, and buoyancy.

In addition to speedskating, I find myself in the world of curling a lot. This is another upper Midwest sport I never would have been a big fan of before but now I find pretty interesting. It's like a giant game of shuffleboard and chess on ice, the idea being to knock the other team's stones out of the main circle. It looks, well, not easy, but not too hard either—until you put on the foot grips and actually try it. I could barely keep my balance to send the stone sputtering down the ice. Once again, my unathletic gene rears its ugly head. It should be one smooth forward motion, with the stone releasing cleanly on a perfect line of travel to its final destination. Then there are "sweepers" trying to move the stone along with broom-like contraptions and one person near the circle at the other end of the ice who is like the director, yelling at his teammates to sweep harder or slower or move it this way or that.

There is a curling club across the street from Lambeau Field. We interviewed the entire men's and women's teams there before Vancouver. They looked like bankers, police officers, and tax accountants because they were. They all had regular jobs that had been put on hold for the Games. I was rooting for them and was especially disappointed when both teams had poor performances that year.

For the Summer Games we talk to runners, basketball players, soccer players, and gymnasts. I find everything about them fascinating and also hard to fathom. Here they have to train for four years for their one chance to perform on the world stage. Yes, many of them also are in world cups and other global events, but the crown jewel is the Olympics and most of them get just this one shot at glory. I have seen heartbreak over the years too many times, including that experienced by runner and Stevens Point native Chris Solinsky. We interviewed him and fellow former Badger Matt Tegenkamp on the UW–Madison campus and got b-roll of them running by Camp Randall. Although they were training together and were friends, they were also rivals attempting to make the US team. Solinsky failed to get out of the US qualifying rounds when

Tegenkamp finished just ahead of him. How hard would it be to wait four more long years after that for another shot? At the next Olympics Solinsky had an injury and couldn't even make it to trials. Tegenkamp went to two Olympics but finished thirteenth in 2008 and nineteenth in 2012, his own form of disappointment.

One of the more memorable interviews I did was with speedskater Nancy Swider-Peltz's mom, Nancy. The older Nancy coached the younger one, which in and of itself creates an interesting dynamic, but I wanted to ask the elder Nancy something else.

"This may sound unusual but I want to start this interview asking you about your bathroom," I said.

"My bathroom?"

I had read that she had inspirational quotes printed on some of the tiles in the shower.

Nancy told me she believes kids are what they absorb around them, so she and her husband came up with the idea to put quotes in the shower that their kids would see every day. When the camera turned to the young Nancy, she was able to recite verbatim some of those quotes, including:

"Far better it is to dare mighty things, to win glorious triumphs, even though checkered by failure, than to rank with those poor spirits who neither enjoy much nor suffer much because they live in the gray twilight that knows neither victory nor defeat."

That one was Teddy Roosevelt. This next one is Lao Tzu:

"Watch your thoughts, they become words. Watch your words, they become actions. Watch your actions, they become habits. Watch your habits, they become character. Watch your character, it becomes your destiny."

I thought the tile idea was a brilliant one and gave it a few whirls in my own head. Would my kids benefit from motivational showers? I'm sure they would, but I still have yet to actually find the time and money to retile ours.

When we were done, Nancy Sr. told me, "Nice interview. Very different kinds of questions." This made me smile. There is nothing better than hearing words like that when you're a reporter because too often it's the other way—you had dumb questions, you were too probing, you weren't probing enough, or you're just a talking airhead who's on TV, a blow-dried, read-the-prompter puppet. Compliments don't come often.

Wrestler Ben Askren was going to compete in the 2008 Summer Games in Beijing. There was a big send-off in Hartland, near Milwaukee, and I was being sent to cover it. Askren had a large chin, sort of Jay Leno-ish, and his family had made funny T-shirts that read "Putting the Chin in China" for everyone to wear. The event itself was lovely—at a country club with balloons and food and Askren's friends. But the day stands out in my mind for a personal tragedy that had nothing to do with Askren or his proud family.

On the way to the event I got a call from my husband that his brother-in-law Randy was in the hospital after a freak bike accident in Minnesota and it didn't look good. I was quite numb doing the happy, going-to-the-Olympics piece and kept checking my phone for any news. I had to man up (or woman up) and do my job. When we got back outside, Paul did call with the devastating update. Randy had died. I remember shock, denial, anger—all of the grief feelings coming in waves. Randy and Paul's sister, Margi, had two young adopted kids and the family had all been together on a bike ride when this happened. I was sick to my stomach. Paul and I went to the funeral later that week, driving in one long day to Mankato, Minnesota. Moments like this reminded me that sports are sports and life is life. Whether you're an Olympic athlete or a normal person, we all go through the same things—births, death, happiness, and tragedies—and all you can do is roll with it.

BEING A WOMAN IN THIS FIELD

PEOPLE SOMETIMES ASK ME if there's an advantage to being a woman in the world of men's sports. I can think of one example of this in particular from early in my career. B. J. Surhoff was the Milwaukee Brewers catcher and his son had autism. I had heard this and wanted to see if Surhoff would be willing to do a story on it, to help bring awareness to a very real disorder.

He wasn't sure. He told me he'd get back to me. Weeks went by and I heard nothing, so I assumed it was off. Then his wife, Polly, called.

"B. J. will do the story. I have to tell you, he only agreed to it because you're a woman," she told me. "He would not have been comfortable talking about this with a man."

The story itself I wish I had done a better job on. I was sick the night we went to his big, suburban house, and I was having trouble getting my head right. We interviewed two autism experts as well as B. J. and his wife. The story was called "Mason's World." B. J. and Polly had made it clear that they wanted the main piece to be about autism, not just about their son. I tried my best to deliver, but the 10:00 producer was not happy with how I put it together. She told me I should not have had an autism expert be the first sound bite. I should have started with the family. Maybe she was right, but I also wanted to deliver what the Surhoffs wanted out of respect for them and their story.

"Your storytelling will get better over time," she said. I was disappointed, but I always felt grateful to B. J. for opening his heart.

Women can and do bring a different perspective to the table. I like to think of my mom and my stepdad when I write a story. My mom knows nothing about sports and only wants the human touch; my stepdad needs to break down Xs and Os. If I can satisfy both, I'm doing my job.

Have there been times we female reporters have used any womanly virtues to get what we want? Yes. And I don't mean sleeping around. I will tell you one story.

The Packers are playing in San Francisco. For some crazy reason our assignment editor has not secured a parking pass. I'm dispatched to the keeper of the passes at Candlestick to essentially beg for one.

"Do whatever you have to do but get a parking pass. We're screwed without one," I'm told.

The parking-pass lord is a large guy with slicked-back black hair. He walks me to his office.

"You guys should have requested one earlier," he tells me. "There's very limited parking. Why should I give it to you?"

Let me cut to the chase here: I proceed to sit in the guy's office chatting and flirting with him for a half hour ("So—how long have you worked here? Where are you from?") before he finally gives me "the last pass."

I go back to my fellow sports anchors.

"You have no idea what I went through for this," I tell them. "You need to thank me for the rest of your lives for taking that bullet."

"Well, we knew none of us had a shot, so we sent you in there."

When we get back to Milwaukee I send a thank-you note to parking-pass guy because we really would have been in deep trouble trying to do a live show without the pass. He writes me back, saying, "I should have asked you out when you were here." Yuck. That's not what I meant. I just wanted to stay on his good side in case we were ever in a dire parking situation again. I didn't enjoy being the pawn in the male-female flirting game, but it was simply something we had to do to park the satellite truck that day and in some weird way I was

proud to be able to contribute when told, "We need this and you have to come through."

Then there are the downsides to being a woman in this field. One night I am covering one of our basketball teams at a tournament out of the state. We decide to interview the game announcer, a high-profile sportscaster, to get his insight into who might win. He's wearing a tie with little handprints on it and after the interview I compliment him on it.

"Thanks. My kids made it for me," he says. I also notice he's wearing a wedding ring and I think to myself, "He seems like a nice dad," which is why it's all the more disheartening when he calls my hotel room that night.

"Hey, is this Jessie? I met you downstairs earlier," he says. "I was just wondering if you'd like to get a drink with me, maybe a little dinner."

Is he making a pass at me? I'm shocked. To cover this embarrassing moment for the both of us, I act as if he's asking both me and my male photographer, Pat, to dinner.

"Oh, thanks, that's really nice, but Pat and I already ate. I appreciate you asking us, though."

I hang up the phone and sit by the window for a bit, just thinking and feeling a little down. Did I do something wrong to lead him on in any way by just being friendly? Was this the norm for reporters on the road or was he just a snake? Or maybe I was reading it wrong—maybe he genuinely wanted to buy a young reporter dinner and offer career advice. But something about it didn't smell right and it made me sad to think that this married father could be putting the moves on many a young woman when he was far from home.

Back in Milwaukee the much older coach of one of our local teams also asks me to dinner. He sends me a box of team stuff. Apparently he got my phone number from another reporter who then laughed and teased me about it. I have to call the coach and thank him and politely decline the invite. I will have to interview this coach many times after this and the subject is never brought up again, but it, too, depresses me a little. I always force a smile around him and act as if it never happened, but I could never forget it. My respect for him was never the same.

Opposite page: My entire goal as a reporter was to bring the human side as well as the factual to the table.

When you're a woman in sports there can be rumors you have no control over. Apparently someone saw someone who looked like me out with a Bucks player one night. From that point forward the guys in the sports office were convinced I was dating this player on the side and chided me endlessly in a joking way, as they knew Paul well. No amount of protesting did any good. I was happy when the player moved on from Milwaukee.

In another incident, my sports director, Dennis Krause, and I had an argument about whether or not I could wear shorts to training camp.

"But all of the guys [male reporters] do it," I protested. "It's hotter than hell and I'm supposed to wear pants?"

"It's different," Dennis insisted. "You're a woman."

We went back and forth on this the whole way up to practice one steamy summer day as I stared out at the passing cornfields angrily. It was only after I grew older that I realized the wisdom of his advice and started watching my clothing more and more. Capri pants were a nice compromise.

Back to the good parts of being a woman in the business. I'm not saying a man wouldn't do or think of these things, but sometimes we're just more tuned in to emotions. Michael Jordan was in town with the Bulls. It was shortly after the Oklahoma City bombing and there was a special moment of silence and playing of the national anthem for the victims. I noticed that Jordan was looking down and wiping his eyes during it. After the game he strode into the press conference exuding confidence and grace. He is one of those people who take over a room. I listened as the Chicago media asked about rebounds, defense, and his ankle. Then I spoke up: "Michael, you seemed to be moved by the pregame ceremony for Oklahoma City. Did that have meaning for you?"

He gave a thoughtful answer that I used on the news that night. One of the Chicago reporters turned and shot me a dirty look, like "what a dumb thing to ask," then jumped right back into asking about the three-point shooting percentage. It was the one and only question I ever asked Jordan in my life. It was the one time I was in a press conference with him. I do not regret asking it as opposed to some stat from some game that nobody remembers. I remember that Jordan was a good person who was emotional along with the rest of America.

WOMEN IN THE LOCKER ROOM

IT'S EASY TO IDENTIFY my worst locker room moment. There are no other contenders.

In the mid-1990s the Cleveland Indians were in town to play the Brewers and I was sent to their clubhouse to get some pregame interviews. The visitors' clubhouse at County Stadium was up some stairs and in a tiny, cramped space. It was actually my first time not covering the home team.

The second I walked in the door the catcalls started.

"Hey, everybody, there's a woman here. Why would a woman come in here? She just wants to see us naked," yells one player I don't even recognize. I feel my cheeks flush and I swallow hard. But I will not be deterred.

"We're here to get interviews," I shoot back at the player.

"Yeah, sure. You just want to see our junk," he says with a laugh, and now the whole Indians team is looking at me. Most of them are laughing as they put on their uniforms, some joining in with whistles or calls of agreement. I feel trapped.

"Just ignore it and let's get one interview and get out of here," says my photographer Chris. He's an older guy, close to retiring, with a direct, no-nonsense way about him. He's seen it all, but I can tell even he is bothered by this.

There is only one player who comes to my defense.

"Come on, guys, leave her alone," says pitcher Orel Hershiser. He's a devout Christian, I remember to myself. Shyly I walk over to Hershiser.

"Would you mind if we talked to you?" I ask. He's not even scheduled to throw that night, but I want to cut our losses and get the hell out of there.

"Sure, no problem." Chris hoists the camera on his shoulder and just as I'm asking Hershiser about the Brewers and the game, the original offender, the guy who yelled when I walked in the door, sneaks up behind Chris. I can see it out of the corner of my eye. He reaches up and turns off a switch on the side of the camera, the viewfinder flickering to darkness.

"Hey, watch it, buddy," says Chris angrily. I have rarely seen him raise his voice, but in this moment his face is red. "Don't you ever touch my camera. You got that?"

"Oooh, big man . . . don't touch my camera," mocks the player. Where are the PR people, the coaches? I am asking myself. I'm starting to feel a little nervousness to go along with my anger. If there is a mob mentality, who is there to protect Chris and me? Hershiser? He can't do it alone. I can tell he's the outcast in this locker room. Chris turns the camera back on and fortunately player jerk backs off, but he's still laughing and encouraging his teammates to keep up the heckling.

"OK, back to the interview," I say. We ask Hershiser about two more lightning-fast questions and hightail it out of there. I thank him several times and he nods in a sad, yes-they're-assholes kind of way.

When Chris and I get outside of the locker room I'm rattled. Tears spring to my eyes.

"What a bunch of complete, sophomoric imbeciles," says Chris with disgust in his voice. I nod in agreement. "You can't let them get away with that." He is emphatic. He was scorned, too.

When we return to the station I tell my boss Dennis about it. He's sympathetic and immediately looks up the number of the Indians PR department. First he talks, then he hands the phone to me. I tell the story.

"Sorry about that," says the guy on the phone. "That's just kind of the way they are. You know, guys being guys. You're not the first one to complain about their behavior, male or female."

Oh, that's just fantastic, I'm thinking. Now they're notorious jerks, but no one is doing anything about it. It's the "boys' network."

"We'll register your complaint, but really it's just a bunch of joking around," says the PR guy. I have a feeling my complaint might go unreported. It seems there are no filters for this group.

I have never had an experience to rival the one with the Indians.

In all of my years covering the Packers there was only one player who refused to be interviewed in the locker room: Reggie White. But he was an equal-opportunity no-interviewee. He would tell the male and female reporters, "You know me, I don't talk in here. I'll be in the hallway in five minutes," and we'd all converge in the small hallway.

Players are in various states of undress when reporters are let in. It's the truth. Some are just stripping to go into the showers; others are just coming back. Some are fully clothed already. Others hide out in the trainers' room if they don't feel like being interviewed. It's a reality in every professional sport. College locker rooms are different; in my experience, they are closed to reporters after a game. Instead, the key guys are brought to a press conference, and you can stand in the hallway for everyone else. Ditto for high school. But professional sports opened their doors to men long ago and needed to do the same for women or risk being sued. And so all reporters crowd in at the same time.

There is a scene in *Jerry Maguire* where the reporter drops her microphone in front of a nude guy and has to bend down in front of him. I have always hated this scene, meant for laughs but which perpetuates a bad stereotype. I have never interviewed any player while he was naked; most guys prefer to be dressed. My personal policy is to turn my back and ask my (almost always male) photographer, "Tell me when he's dressed," before I approach a player.

Today, professional football, basketball, hockey, and baseball players are more or less used to women in the locker room. Back in those Cleveland Indians days, women were still just starting in the business. Now we're so common, the players don't blink. I have interviewed many a player who was wearing shorts and nothing else, but it was absolutely no big deal. My feeling is if you show them respect, they will do the same. If I were to look them up and down or flirt it would be a different story. If I were to come to the scene in high heels and a skintight skirt or a see-through top it might be different, but I have always dressed professionally and never felt out of place—except this one other time that was so unexpected I still have a hard time believing it happened.

The Brewers were closing in on the 2011 playoffs. We were down at Miller Park a lot. I was in the clubhouse interviewing Prince Fielder with a group of other reporters when another player made a loud noise behind us—so loud that we all turned around. And there he was, in his birthday suit with his arms outstretched, laughing.

"Yeah, how about that?" he yelled. Flustered, we all turned back to Fielder with nervous laughs. We carried on with the interview and nothing else happened, but I could never look at that player the same way again. What had possessed him to do that? He was a family man whom I had seen with his wife and kids several times. When I told my husband what happened he was shocked as well.

"Are you serious? I never thought of him that way," he said.

"How were the Brewers today?" my older son asked. "Did you interview [the player who did this]?"

"No, not today," I replied, the image of him flashing into my mind. I never told my kids. I didn't want them to think less of one of their heroes.

PACKERS AND
PLAY-DOH

FOR FOURTEEN YEARS I will juggle motherhood and sportscasting. It isn't easy. When people ask me what I do I say, "It's either Packers or Play-Doh, sometimes both at the same time." There are moments when I have to laugh at myself. I'm changing a diaper and studying the Packers media guide simultaneously, trying to get ready for sideline reporting duties. I smear on Desitin, while checking to see where Ryan Grant went to high school.

One night in the middle of my most intense years of sideline reporting, Paul and I get a rare and much needed night out. We find an outdoor restaurant and settle in to order appetizers, but I am way behind in preparing for an interview the next day.

"Honey, please don't be mad at me. Do you mind if I just write down a few questions and look up a couple of things while we're waiting for our food?" I ask. "I haven't had any time with the kids being off from school."

"Oh, sure, go ahead and ruin our date with a Packers player," he says with a laugh, but he's patiently quiet for a few minutes so I can do my work while we both nibble on bruschetta.

When Jake is a tiny baby and I am nursing him, I have to take him to Lambeau to shoot a one-hour special for *Inside 1265*. Paul is still on paternity leave and comes along to hold Jake. As the camera is being set up on the 20-yard line, Jake starts screaming. He needs to be fed and changed. Yikes! I take him into the Packers tunnel and start the process. First a new diaper, then nursing, then check the diaper again. Paul takes a picture of me changing Jake in the tunnel, then holds and rocks him until I'm done saying the memorized lines. I'm speaking the words I need to speak, but I'm watching Paul and our baby out of the corner of my eye and I'm on edge in case he starts crying again while the tape is running. When we finish, we put his car seat on the field and take a picture to show him someday that he got to be on the Packers 50!

Another time I have to take Jake to Lambeau alone. Paul can't go and my mom has something else happening. I budget in lots of extra driving time knowing I will have to stop several times each way to feed him. He's still pretty small. Our producer watches over him this time while

Yup, there's my little bundle the day we dragged him to Lambeau Field for a shoot. I also think I might be the first person to have changed a diaper in the tunnel.

I shoot standups. Then I have to record some lines into the camera so they can edit a piece. Here's the funny part: every time I start talking, Jake starts fussing. We stop, we start, he fusses, we laugh, we stop, we start. I'm trying to read fast so I can get the line in before the next fuss. The photographer has three kids and is extremely patient. Finally I get a bottle out, put Jake in my arms, and read my lines with an infant sucking away in my arms. No one would know because it is only my voice being recorded at this time.

A few weeks later we are in the middle of taping *Inside 1265*, when the crew throws a football to Larry McCarren, who then hands it to me. The Packers equipment manager had hand painted a football with "Congratulations on the birth of future Packer Jacob Logan Marble. See ya at Lambeau in 20 years." It's a complete surprise and something that has a place of honor on Jake's dresser still.

One year I was asked to speak at Miller Brewing Company about the challenges of working and parenting. Paul told me he could be home by 4:00 no problem and I'd be free to get to my talk by 5:00. As you've probably guessed, he called at 3:30 saying he was so sorry, but there was no way he'd be back on time. I had no backup plan (hadn't I learned anything yet about Murphy's Law?), so I packed up preschooler Jake and took him, and his Curious George playhouse, with me. As I stepped onto the stage I told the audience I just needed a moment to get George and The Man with the Yellow Hat set and I'd be ready to talk. This was, after all, a perfect example of my topic.

Charlie had a speech delay as a toddler and my focus turned to helping him. A speech therapist came to our house once a week and we enrolled him in a birth-to-three program that included integration into a special preschool class with speech and occupational therapists. We practiced with games and flash cards the speech therapist provided. I started turning down nearly all of the requests that came my way, from emceeing high-powered lunches to talking sports with local church groups, especially if the time involved took me from the house while Charlie was home. I felt I needed to be there to assist with his learning as much as possible. The only people I was comfortable leaving him with were my mom and a wonderful matronly babysitter we found who would make blankets for both boys and had endless patience and sweetness. Charlie slowly grew out of his delay, but I was so grateful I could facilitate his care when he needed it.

There were times I loved being Laura Ingalls Wilder, pioneer woman,

Paul would often bring Jake in for dinner while I was working.

growing my own veggies and making do with less (a.k.a. working fewer hours), all while balancing a baby on my hip. And there were days I longed to be Katie Couric, career woman, being rushed off to work in a limo in my high heels and interviewing George Clooney.

I want to stay home with my kids/want to work/want to stay home/want to work. I can't afford to stay home, that's the bottom line. We need two incomes because my husband is not a doctor or a lawyer: he's a photographer—an excellent one who is creative and engaged and loves his job. The truth is I like being in the adult world, too. There are not enough words to describe my affection for my kids—I often tell them, "I love you mountains and rivers and oceans and canyons"—but I find building block towers and watching them fall mind-numbing despite all of my pretend enthusiasm. I get so bored on the floor playing with bright-colored plastic all the time that I try to perfect the art of *Chopsticks* on the Fisher-Price piano.

I feel more alive and the day goes a lot faster when I'm working, but I also cherish being home. Watching my boys learn to climb or read, answering their many questions, like "Does everyone have lungs?" is so satisfying and brings me such joy. Even the simple things, like hearing Charlie babbling on the baby monitor, turn my whole stomach warm and mushy every time. Plus, the household just runs more smoothly if I'm not working. My husband forgets to check the boys' backpacks, where important papers are completely overlooked until I dig them out at midnight, and where their lunch boxes fester, unwashed.

During my early working years, I always knew I wanted to be a mother. It was such a deep primal need it would overtake all else. It took us eight months of trying before Jake. I was like an astronaut turbo-launched to the moon with joy, but I also fully expected to go back to work full time because my job meant everything to me. My own mother had worked full time, as did my friends' mothers. I couldn't remember one stay-at-home mom from my childhood.

"I'll just put the kid in day care," I confidently told my boss.

"OK—first of all, you won't be calling it 'the kid' for very long," the father of two said patiently. "Secondly, you might change your mind when you see your baby."

How right he was. The moment Jake came into the world—blinking at us from his hospital bassinet—my very existence as I knew it was shaken like a snow globe. Those first few months of motherhood were akin to having everything you ever thought about your life crumpled up and thrown over the side of the Grand Canyon. And I adored him. How could I put this tiny creature in full-time day care? I first requested to drop to four days a week, then three days a week, then finally I became the "floater" in the department, working part time and filling in when needed. I gave up a lot of money, not to mention the prestige of climbing the career ladder. We stayed in our little three-bedroom house. We lived with the refrigerator that had duct tape holding two of the drawers together. But to have that little person curled up on your lap—there was no greater joy.

We paced ourselves, and saved up for things, and I found it surprisingly rewarding to be a little patient. I want to make a smaller footprint on the environment anyway, so I asked myself if that large-screen TV was really necessary? Could I ride my bike and save a little gas? Could I shop at rummage sales instead of Baby Gap? The answer was a 100 percent resounding yes. The reward of time with my family was priceless, and my boys' childhood was something I could never get back.

When Charlie made us a family of four, both the love and the craziness in the house increased. I would play peekaboo with him all morning, taking a cursory glance at the sports pages when I could. I would be so tired I'd stumble through the day longing for multiple Diet Cokes but not getting any because I was nursing. I would wear pink on the air with

With Charlie at our favorite vacation spot in Door County

the thought that it might make me look a little more cheery and alert than I actually was. I would work my night shift, dealing with producers and editors and being responsible for three sportscasts while dashing off to the ladies' room to pump breast milk when I could. I would return home and invariably have to nurse Charlie sometime during the night, staring blankly at the rotating night light I had looked at so many times I knew its every curve.

One Fourth of July epitomized my life trying to balance kids, Paul's work, and my responsibilities.

It had started a few weeks earlier when Jake had a new bug catcher. He and I were just securing ant number eight into its new grassless world, when a woman I knew rode up on her bike.

"Jessie, hi!" she called over. "Did you know I'm in charge of the Fourth of July parade? We're looking for a local celebrity to ride in the back of a sports car. You'd be willing to do that, wouldn't you?"

"Uhhh . . ." I'm stalling. I love watching parades but not being in them. I always feel like a fish in a bowl or a monkey in a cage. Yet if I say no, am I uncaring about my community?

"Mommy, can I be in the parade?" Jake's voice is squealing with excitement. Rats! Foiled by the four-year-old.

"OK, I guess you got me. Jake and I will be in it together," I say with a sigh and smile at him as he jumps up and down.

The big day arrives and it couldn't be off to a worse start. Huge storms rolled through, waking us all up way too early and knocking out power. The parade starts at 9:00. I take a shower and only then realize that I will not have a blow-dryer. My hair with no dryer, especially on a humid day, will be a big ball of frizz. I towel dry it as best I can, rushing around to get Charlie changed and ready for my parents, who have come in from Madison to watch him.

"Mommy, let's go! We can't be late!" Jake is beyond excited. I glance at my wardrobe, then at the thermometer outside the kitchen window. Ninety degrees. Ugh. A red T-shirt is all that is clean and somewhat patriotic-looking. I put that on, my hair still damp and starting to curl up the way I detest. I feel fat; "Body by Jake and Charlie" is a T-shirt I think I should own. Will black pants make me look slimmer? I pull those on and Jake is yanking my hand out the door.

"There's a bottle in the fridge," I call to my parents. "See you on the parade route."

Jake and I scurry to the start. We're placed in the back of a car with a giant magnetic name tag proclaiming who I am on the side. There is also a huge bag of mini plastic footballs that I'm expected to throw at the kids in the crowd. Our station's logo is on each one. I take a deep breath and try to forget the fact that I feel chubby, messy, tired. Smile big, girl.

Jake and I use up all of the footballs by the time the parade is half-way done. He loves waving at everyone; I endure it. The station has sent a photographer to get video of us and I smile but make a silent vow to myself not to do this again. I would much prefer to be sitting with everyone else on the curb. The temperature is really rising and I'm sweating to go with the bad hair. My husband would be here as moral support except for one thing: when the power went out he was called in. There is storm damage and he needs to go with a news reporter to shoot video and interviews.

The parade is finally done, the organizer has thanked me several times, and we can be on our way. The power is still out at home and the house is getting crazy-hot with no air-conditioning. My parents have to go—they have plans with some of their friends back in Madison. My mom reluctantly says good-bye.

Paul calls to check in on me and to say that he'll be gone at least another three hours. Now things are getting really uncomfortable on the first floor and especially on the second—there's that feeling of heavy air not circulating. We're all sweating. Charlie needs to nap. Jake needs to nap but probably won't. I need a nap.

I take the whole herd, cats included, to the basement where the cool air that we can't stand in the wintertime now feels delightful. I grab our old camping cooler (the one Paul and I used as a young couple when we would stay up late at the campfire listening to Brewers games and sipping beers) and fill it with ice from the quickly melting freezer, throw a few drinks in, and we're all set up for the rest of the morning. I play a few rounds of Candy Land with Jake while watching Charlie roll around on his bright red mat. We all have a snack and I get the whole lot of us to lie down on the guest bed we keep in the basement.

"OK, guys—let's try to sleep."

Amazingly, with a little nursing, Charlie conks right out. I am stunned to look over at Jake on the bed and see him breathing deeply. It's a miracle! I have two sleeping children! This is the best damn Fourth of July in history! I close my eyes, too, knowing this will be a lifesaving nap. I open one eye and peek over at my two little people, their eyelids fluttering, and I feel a rush of love. I am still wowed by the fact that as a human race we create other humans. How is it possible that these people came from me, that I am responsible for their existence? Their eyelashes, their toes, everything seems magical to me. As my mother once described it, "Being a parent is like walking around with your heart outside your body." When we wake up, Paul is home and he and I chalk up our morning to another in the long line of experiences that make up parenting.

As the kids got older we started bringing them to Green Bay when I had to sideline report. We could almost never actually get tickets to the game, as Packers tickets are like chunks of gold, but they would come and swim in the hotel, go out to eat, and watch the game from either a sports restaurant or the hotel room. The kids loved the little getaway; I loved being able to see them. They would come to *The Mike McCarthy Show* with me once a year and were able to shake hands with Coach and take a picture with him. One year Jake brought along two friends. I could see they were feeling sheepish as McCarthy made small talk with all of them; their voices were a little softer and they looked up at him with awe. Later, though, they couldn't stop talking about the experience.

My kids were already huge fans of the team—it seems green and gold pulses through their veins, as it does for so many people in Wisconsin—but this may have solidified their fervor. If they were ever wowed by their mom on television, they never showed it. They might ask, "Who was the guest [on *The Mike McCarthy Show*] today?" And if I were to say "Clay Matthews" or "Aaron Rodgers," they would respond, "Cool," but that was it. It was a job and, in fact, became a tiresome one, especially for Charlie. "It's not Monday again! *Awww* . . . ," he would say, knowing that Mondays meant I would be in Green Bay sometimes past his bedtime. Other kids at school were much more impressed. "I saw you on TV last night!" random children might say as I worked in the school library on a day off. A mother once told me her kindergartner recognized me but then got mad because I wasn't responding to his greeting through the television screen.

After one particularly muggy sideline reporting game, I was back in the hotel room and looking forward to a good night's sleep. I needed it because the next day I had to cover the PGA Championship at Whistling Straits near Kohler. Whistling Straits sits right on Lake Michigan. It's a stunning place that rises up out of flat cornfields to make you feel like you're in Scotland. Rolling hills, a wicked breeze off the lake, amazing water views—it is impressive. All the big stars were there and I had to cover the final round on Sunday. Only one thing: Paul and the boys were with me and Charlie had a cough, and he hacked all night long. He had asked me to sleep in his bed with him, so I curled up around him as best I could. Not only was he coughing but he was also thrashing around on the small hotel bed. I would just start to drift off when he would either cough or flop around like a sputtering fish. I didn't want to

Next pages: Mike McCarthy was very gracious meeting my kids and their friends after a show taping. COURTESY OF DEAN MUELLER

wake anyone else, but I could not stay on the bed with him, so I wound up on the floor. A torture chamber could not be much worse. You're on the hardest surface in the world with your head right next to a grubby carpet that you know has been walked on by thousands of strangers. You're wrapped in that thin hotel blanket trying to keep warm, and your little one is in bed a few feet away and, in your tired opinion, making more noise than a landing airplane. The noise seemed not to affect Paul and Jake, who were blissfully in la-la land. Next morning I woke up (if I ever fell asleep) stiff and sore and tired as heck but managed to work a twelve-hour shift.

Another moment in parenting history.

That day, while interviewing Tiger Woods, Phil Mickelson, and Steve Stricker, I also worried about Charlie's cough. I called Paul several times, relieved to find Charlie was playing basketball back in our driveway, feeling better after what he perceived as a good night's sleep.

At least one of us could say that.

Understatement of the century: life as a mom is hard. So hard that I pitch an idea to the station to do a nonsports segment each week called "4 Your Family." We will do stories on anything related to kids and families. It's a refreshing change from sports, and the segment runs for several years with stories ranging from same-sex parents, grandparents as parents, and homeschooling to how to find the right sunscreen/dentist/doctor/shoe store and the great vaccination debate. I was just starting to be known for family stories as well as sports when the station decided to cancel "4 Your Family." It was taking too much time to write and produce these segments every week. I couldn't argue, but I missed working on the pieces. Combining journalism and family was something that had clicked. It felt right. I was able to see how other people managed their lives with kids and to pick up helpful parenting tips. In time, though, it started to dawn on me that, despite my best efforts at going part time, something was off-kilter in my own life.

CHANGES

HOW MANY PEOPLE have to miss Christmas and New Year's and every other major holiday on a regular basis to work? The news never stops, ever. The Packers often play on big holidays so more people will tune in, which means I am stuck at home while Paul takes the kids to Minneapolis for Christmas with his family two years in a row. With his thirteen brothers and sisters producing thirty-five cousins for my kids, it's a rocking good time that has to take place at a hotel. No one has the space for that many people at their house.

They all reserve rooms for the night. The kids splash in the pool and chase each other around the hallways. The good Minnesotans each make a "hot dish" to share and the family eats in one of the hotel banquet rooms. It's a tradition the kids look forward to. Of course they should go. But I have to stay.

It's "all hands on deck" when the Packers play. The first year I anchor on both Christmas Eve and Christmas Day. People at the station have a potluck on Christmas Eve, and there is a merry feeling, despite the work. But Christmas Day I wake up and think "Most of the rest of the world is opening presents around the tree right now." I get myself a bowl of cold cereal.

There is not much food in the house. I figure I can stop at our local grocery store and pick up a salad from the salad bar for lunch. When I get there it's closed. So is the other grocery store and every gas station, restaurant, and fast-food place in town. Not even McDonald's?

I turn the car around and go back home to scrounge for whatever I can. There is a can of soup at the back of the cupboard. This will be lunch. A couple of packets of instant oatmeal will be dinner. I take them with me to the station, now truly feeling sorry for myself. The kids call from the hotel. There is laughter in the background; they're playing board games with their cousins. My heart is heavy. I can't do this anymore.

It dawns on me that my older child will be thirteen in the spring. Only five more Christmases until he's off to college. Only three years until he gets his driver's license. He's already starting to pull away from family toward friends. His brother is still in the active mom-and-dad stage, but I can see now how fleeting that is, and I don't want to be saying "Mommy has to work" on Saturdays and holidays anymore. Then, of course, Charlie will be on his way someday, too, and Paul and I will be left to figure out what life looks like without the pandemonium of parenting. When that time comes I will have all day to work as much as I want. For now, I simply need more of my day devoted to the home front.

One night driving home from Green Bay I think of my college roommate and maid of honor, Adriana, who had recently passed away after a ten-year battle with breast cancer. Her death reminded me how transient we all are on this earth. I was so shaken by losing her at the age of forty-one that I saw a counselor for a while afterward. She advised me to talk directly to Adriana, as I likely knew what she would say in any situation. We could practically carry on a two-way conversation, the counselor explained. So now I tentatively try it somewhere near Manitowoc and ask Adriana what she thinks I should do career-wise, and suddenly her voice pops loud and clear into my head.

"I always thought that was a crazy-ass job," I hear her say in her usual direct and humorous way. "Get out." My eyes fill with tears as I silently thank Adriana and tell her for about the zillionth time how much I miss her.

It's time for a tweak in the job. Twenty years of sportscasting and I'm ready to make some changes. I think of the John Lennon song "Watching the Wheels."

"No longer riding on the merry-go-rou-ound. I just had to let it go."
His words hit home.

I look at the other female anchors around town and suddenly notice a trend. Nearly all of the night shift anchors and reporters have either no children or grown ones. There are a scant few of us trying to make it work with a young family. Even the male anchors and reporters don't often have small kids. Those television people who do have made many changes to try to accommodate their lives as working parents. Our two morning-show anchors *asked* to be on a shift that would require them to go to bed at 7:30 p.m., rise at 2:00 a.m., and be on the air at 5:00 a.m. so they can be home at a reasonable hour and help with all of their family's night routines. Other than the two of them, though, I have seen countless talented people leave the business looking for better hours—not to mention more pay (television does not pay well unless you're one of the main honchos).

Men can age well on the air. A little gray in the sideburns is attractive, distinguished. But women? You see gray in their hair on-screen and you might gasp. Why do you think Joan Rivers does what she does? The aging process is hard on women and some will do just about anything to stop it. I don't want to be forced to undergo plastic surgery someday. I want to age naturally, warts and all.

Fame, even a little bit, can do funny things to people. It's really the rare person who doesn't let it go to his or her head at some point. I always thought that when your name was bigger than you were it was time to slow down a bit. I've seen many athletes and celebrities have a love/hate relationship with fame. "Yes, you all can love me/No, get the heck away from me. I want everyone to recognize me/I want no one to recognize me." Celebrities have drug problems, I've always thought, because they need a place to escape. Finding the right balance is tricky. I need to make each side of my own scale dangle at equal levels for my sanity, Paul's, and the kids'.

I tell the news director and general manager that I need to change my hours. I hug the boys at the Greyhound station as they go off with Paul, yet again, without me to Minneapolis for a second Christmas.

My three favorite guys. This was taken at a Phillies spring training game in Florida during spring break.

"This is the last time," I say. I mean it.

Will I miss the excitement of Packers games? Of traveling the country? Yes. Will I miss being recognized on the street, worrying about hair and makeup, getting home late and being aware at all moments that people could be criticizing me? Not one bit. I strike a deal with the station management. I will work in a limited capacity. I ask to give up *The Mike McCarthy Show* and sideline reporting, but I will be available periodically for small assignments. In the meantime, I scratch an itch that's been there a long time by taking a teaching job at a local university. I'm looking forward to passing something on and to being in the academic world. I will be an adjunct professor, instructing upper-level students in broadcast news reporting. If I'm going to be honest with them and myself about the business, I need to reflect on a few of the not-so-great memories.

Regrets . . . I've had a few. OK, maybe more than a few, but that will happen when you work in live television for twenty years. It seems like the details of the bad moments are easier to recall than the times when you actually got it right or did it well. The work of television newscasters is so public. We do our best, but, yes, we make mistakes sometimes.

I'm willing to bet everyone has had an error or two at work, but most don't have it go out over the airwaves or, worse, YouTube.

I have had several occasions when I forgot what I was going to say during a live shot and many more times when I nearly forgot what I was going to say but recovered in enough time for no one to notice. We've had the teleprompter go out occasionally and I've had to ad-lib over highlights, which is not easy, even if you've just written the story on your computer in the sports office, because your brain is in overdrive trying to recall all of the players, what the score is, etc. That is the nature of live television, when you're doing dozens of live shots in a week and trying to write and remember everything without constantly referring to your notes. Some TV people are better at it than others. It's an art to look at the black camera lens and be natural and comfortable and informative and conversational all at once.

There have been many times I have second-guessed myself for things. During the height of the Brett Favre retirement-unretirement era, I poked a little fun at him on the air and a woman wrote the station ripping me for my lack of class and for doing this to a "Wisconsin treasure." I wrote back saying I meant no malice and we all respected what Favre had done and she was entitled to her opinion. I ended with, "Thank you for watching and taking the time to write." I never heard back from her.

So what have I learned in my twenty years? I learned that athletes are just people—people with a lot of money, but people, nonetheless. When sports fans ask me what it's like to interview Brett Favre, Aaron Rodgers, Charles Woodson, I shrug. They're people. And they have short careers. They are fleeting. I feel for them. Imagine being told at the age of thirty-five that you're washed up in whatever your passion is. It's no wonder some of them have a hard time after their athletic abilities start to be tested by time.

I learned that your heroes are not quite so large when you meet them in person. While growing up, I had a huge crush on Paul Molitor. The first time I met him for an interview I was still a little butterfly-ish, but he couldn't have been more gracious and kind. Yet, I also realized that he's just a normal person, not a superhuman.

My mom always had a thing for Paul Newman (not New-man). When I told her I interviewed him at a race she caught her breath.

"Really? Paul Newman? Really?"

"Yeah. But, Mom, he just seemed like a short, regular guy."

I also learned that sports is sports and the sun will come up tomorrow. My kids haven't learned this yet. They cry and get mad when their teams lose. Perspective will come.

I learned that family comes first. As I told the GM when I met him in his sunny corner office to declare my departure, my head crammed with emotions about leaving and staying and working and mothering, "I love the Packers, but I love my family more."

I learned that sportscasting is fun and being a woman in this field is rewarding. I enjoyed changing people's minds about women reporting sports, enjoyed telling a good story and feeling good about it. I enjoyed sharing with viewers the best parts of a game or a behind-the-scenes look at someone they saw competing or coaching.

When Ron Wolf left the Packers he said, "You just know when it's time." I'm no Ron Wolf, but I, too, know.

It's time.

I have a few anxious moments. Am I making the right decision? Will I regret this?

When I get home the night after speaking with the GM I look at Jake and Charlie and my heartstrings tug. I will work while they're in school. I will be at every soccer game, noisy band concert, and cute play they have. I haven't been to a football game as a spectator in at least fifteen years, haven't watched a game without taking notes in that time. Paul can go running with earbuds in while the action plays out on the TV. I want to be able to do that, too. Or maybe I'll do the dishes, rake the leaves. Then I can get a drink, make a fire, snuggle, watch the game, watch the kids, watch the wheels.

I just had to let it go.

ACKNOWLEDGMENTS

IN TELEVISION EVERY PERSON YOU SEE on the air has countless others behind the scenes, and so it is in creating a book. I am eternally grateful to Kate Thompson and Kathy Borkowski and the entire team at the Wisconsin Historical Society Press for recognizing potential in this project and editor Laura Kearney for expertly guiding a first-time author through the process. Laura has a great eye and knew just the direction to push me in. Thanks, too, to Diane Drexler, Kristin Gilpatrick, Anna Wehrwein, John Nondorf, editorial intern/Packers owner Shaun Miller, and Katherine Pickett for their efforts on this book.

To my mother, Judy, and stepfather, Howard: thank you for giving me roots, independence, and a love of the written word. I thought poring over a book at the breakfast table and receiving two newspapers a day at your doorstep was just the way everyone lived.

We all need a warm circle of people surrounding us and I am blessed beyond words to have friends who bolster me: Sarah Damonte Vegas, Lauren Fox, Julianne Maggiore, Lori Nickel, and Sarah Scott. Although none of them would ever don a cheerleader's outfit, I often imagined them—pom-poms in hand—as my own personal cheering section. And to Adriana—my fun-loving, sports-averse maid of honor who once came with me to Lambeau Field and read a stack of fashion magazines during a game—I miss you. You still visit me at the most unexpected times of day, and at night in dreams that leave me in tears.

Special thanks to journalist Joel Dresang and author Tim Hansmann, who took time out of their busy schedules to read early drafts of this book and offered spot-on insights. I owe a debt of gratitude to the many WTMJ photographers and to executive sports producer Rick Rietbrock, who listened to various chapters and helped jog my memory countless times as we barreled north on I-43 on our way to yet another Packers practice or game.

The University of Wisconsin–Milwaukee writers' conference and creative nonfiction class were both sources of inspiration and motivation at just the right time.

I am eternally grateful to those who contributed pictures for this book: Jim Angeli, Jim Biever, John Biever, Vern Biever, Rod Burks, the FitzRandoph family, Mark Hoffman, Dean Mueller, and the kids and staff at Indian Hill School, including photographer Kristen Ricigliano. WTMJ graphic artist Steve Armendariz was a godsend and patiently helped me put many images from video into proper format for this book time and again.

Thank you to the players and coaches I covered over the years— especially those who didn't mind being real human beings through it all.

Jake and Charlie: there is simply no way to express my love. You won't understand it unless you become parents yourselves. I hope you look back on your childhood with affection. I can't wait to be a grandma (but no pressure . . . and don't have kids too soon . . . and only if you want to . . .). See how hard it is to say all the right things all the time?

And finally, to Paul—who has been with me for more than half the years I have lived on this planet—I love you and I still get butterflies when I see on my cell phone that it is you calling. There's a line from the movie *High Fidelity* that I have always liked: "It's a mystery of human chemistry and I don't understand it; some people, as far as your senses are concerned, just feel like home." To me, that has always been Paul.

INDEX

Note: Page numbers in *italics* indicate illustrations.

ABOUT THE AUTHOR

MADISON NATIVE Jessie Garcia has been a TV sportscaster for twenty years, first with WISC in Madison and currently with WTMJ in Milwaukee. A graduate of the Boston University College of Communication, Garcia was one of the first women in the country to host an NFL coach's show. When not reporting or anchoring for WTMJ, Garcia can be found teaching journalism, writing her next two books, or enjoying time with her husband and their two sons.